THE JEWISH CHRISTIAN
1

DR. DAVID SPOON

The Jewish Christian

Copyright © 2024 Dr. David Spoon

ISBN: 9798224926497

All rights reserved. No part of this publication may
 be reproduced, stored in, or introduced into a
retrieval system or transmitted in any form or by

any means (electronic, mechanical, photocopying,

recording, or otherwise) without the prior written
permission of the copyright owner. Any person
who does any unauthorized act in relation to this
 publication may be liable to criminal
prosecution and civil claims for damages.

Dedication

I dedicate this book, FIRST, to God Almighty (The Father, Son, and Holy Spirit) for allowing me to get to know You a little more.

I dedicate this book to the best soul I have ever known, my wife and best friend, Noelle.

I dedicate this book to the Hecox family, the Spoon family, the Schiller family, and to my radio family.

And finally, I dedicate this book to each of you who know Him and know that you want more of Him.

You understand a little bit about Moses when he asked for more after all that time with God. "Show me Your glory," he petitioned.

The closer we get to Him, the more we come to understand how far away we are. And how we so hunger to be with Him for all eternity.

Introduction

I am sick of so many books. They often have a smug attitude that comes from a smug author. Or they are so technical that we want to shred them. Or so boring that we want to use them for kindling.

Or so stupid that we feel dumber for reading them.

So, what makes this book different? You.

On this earthly journey, where you are will determine your appreciation or disgust for this book. I cannot promise you a rose garden when you read it (*if you read it at all*). I'm not too fond of gardening. You wouldn't want a rose from me anyway.

I can promise you this: you will read about a fresh perspective on life. It will not be a mathematical perspective or a scientific one. It will not be a pious one or a self-actualization one. It will be a fresh perspective from this Jewish Christian.

This book is not a brilliant piece of literature. I'm blessed that I have a spell check so that I can spell literature. This book is the first in a series; we think, we hope, and we pray.

What makes me so different? My mom would have said, "Because you're the baby in the family." My brother and sister would disagree. So would my wife, although she may agree that I am a baby.

Here's the deal. I was born and raised in a Detroit Jewish home. But unfortunately, I became a purveyor of recreational pharmaceuticals (a small-time drug dealer and drug abuser). I almost died at various times. And I was headed for certain destruction.

But a light came into my life. And I became new. This book is a manifestation of that light and of that new. I hope it blesses you. But if you need to use it for kindling, light it at the bottom first.

Contents

Dedication iii

1 The Foundation of Our Faith 1

2 The Foundation of Our Faith, Part 2 13

3 The Highest Calling 29

4 Sorry God 49

5 The Pursuit of Happiness 69

6 There is No Secret… 85

7 The Jehoshaphat Jam 99

8 Pathways to His Presence 117

9 From Bad to Rad 129

10 Finding the Will of God 155

The Lawsuit Gospel 175

About this Jewish Christian 189

Also, by David Spoon 191

1

The Foundation of Our Faith

I want to talk about the three most famous Scriptures wrongly quoted by people around the world.

The first is *that money is the root of all evil.* That is the most famous quoted Scripture. The only problem? It is not a scripture. The person who said it was Louisa May Alcott— not Jesus Christ, not the Holy Spirit, not God the Father. None of the prophets said it. Louisa May Alcott said it. People don't bother to take the time to read the actual verse in the Bible, where it says **the love** *of money is the root of all evil.* From *money, which is the root of all evil,* came a string of Christian teachings that people should be poor. An entire movement was created from a fake Bible verse.

The second is *that cleanliness is next to godliness.* How often is that quoted on television by people who have pictures of their kids and all that other stuff? Right on the wall, and right next to all that, they have a decorative sign on the wall that says *cleanliness is next to godliness*. It's a great excuse parents use to make their kids clean the room. But Francis Bacon was the person who came up with *cleanliness, which is next to godliness*, not Jesus Christ. A lot of people live by this fake verse, though. They raise their kids with it. They swear by it.

The third is my choice for the most wicked. It was by Algernon Sydney. *God helps those who help themselves*. Let me tell you the damage that this fake scripture has done.

That Scripture has created a works-based theology, thereby misleading millions of people. At one point, Algernon, who was somewhat of a theologian, just didn't feel like having to take care of other peoples' things and came up with the idea that *God helps those that help themselves*. Can you help me move? Sorry, *God helps those who help themselves*. Go move. I don't want to do it.

People use these fake passages of Scripture, and it blows my mind. They aren't anywhere in the Bible.

Let's look at Hosea, chapter four. I just want to explain to you specifically why the authentic people of God are not responding to people who use these fake Scriptures. The people of God are saying nothing. Here's Hosea 4:6:

> *My people are destroyed from lack of knowledge.*

Do you know why Christians don't respond? Because they lack knowledge. We don't know the Bible well enough to be able to respond and say, "What? That is not even in there. "Cleanliness is next to godliness" doesn't exist in this book. "God helps those who help themselves is not a Scripture." People say, "Oh, no, it is a Scripture. I am sure it is in the Bible, and the Martians wrote the Bible. Didn't you know that?" People say the dumbest things, but nobody is responding. Nobody is taking the challenge.

What is the challenge? In Acts 17:10, we learn the kind of people that we are supposed to be. It says this:

> *As soon as it was night, the brothers sent Paul and Silas away to Berea. On arriving there, they went to the Jewish synagogue. Now the Bereans were of more noble character than the Thessalonians, for they received the message with great eagerness and examined the Scriptures every day to see if what Paul said was true.*

Let me tell you what God requires of us. God requires us to be diligent in the Word. And every day, we are required to examine and read it closely. Some of you reading this might be thinking, "Dave, it is boring to read that book." And my response is that I get it.

It is so much fun to read <u>every other book in the universe</u> except for that book. Don't you think there is a reason that you have to struggle to read the Bible? How hard is it to read a book about a mystery with cats and murders? That is my wife. She loves those kinds of books. She reads them all the time. But she has to fight hard to read the Bible. She has to labor. Why? Because it is spiritual warfare. The devil doesn't want you reading the Bible.

But we are supposed to be the type of people who are diligent in the Scriptures every day. When we're diligent and hear somebody say something we know to be false, we'll be ready with the correct response. We are supposed to be quality thinkers.

I want to tell you a story. It's a true story. Occasionally, I flip through the cable news stations and check some of the conservative and non-conservative stations. I think it's interesting. I want to know what everyone is talking about. One time, I came across a channel (which will remain nameless), and the host was talking excitedly because he was about to interview a Bible scholar. I love Bible scholars, too. So now **I'm** excited. I think to myself, "He's a Bible scholar. He's not going to be an idiot. He's going to say something good. It's going to be good information."

The scholar was from Princeton University and had a double Ph.D. **This was going to be great**. He was sitting there, talking to Chris Matthews, and I was listening. I knew something good was coming. It had to be. He was talking to Chris Matthews, and they were talking about Christians, and then the guy says, "Well, Jesus didn't actually claim to be the Messiah."

I must have looked at my TV for a good 30 seconds, just looking at it and thinking, thinking...what? What?! You are a Bible scholar with a double Ph.D., and you're saying that Jesus didn't actually claim to be the Messiah. I can't express the thoughts that were running through my mind at that moment because I will have to repent for them, but I thought, "Man, are you dumb." I couldn't believe it. The answer to this tragedy is found in John 4:25:

> *The woman said to him, "I know that Messiah is coming" (who is called Christ). "When He comes, He will tell us all things." So Jesus said*

> *to her, "I who speak to you am He."*

How much clearer could you get? But the "scholar" claims Jesus never said that. So, what book is he reading? What is going on here? This is the kind of stuff that we need to be aware of every single day.

Look at 2 Peter 3:15-16:

> *Bear in mind that our Lord's patience means salvation, just as our dear brother Paul also wrote you with the wisdom that God gave him. He writes the same way in all his letters, speaking in them about these matters. Nevertheless, his letters contain some things that are hard to understand, which ignorant and unstable people distort to their own destruction as they do the other Scriptures.*

We might think, "Well, do people really do this?" Do you think that David Koresh didn't know the parts of the Bible he knew? He did. He just knew **certain parts**. He was so focused on just those certain parts; he could quote them left and right. But he was so unstable, and he distorted the Scriptures to his own death. So, when we read the book, it needs to be the *whole* book. But, most of all, it needs to be nothing but the book. Because that is where we find the answers, and that is where we get the truth.

Why do we need to know all of it? I am going to show you a surprise from Matthew 4:1-7:

> *Then Jesus was led by the Spirit into the wilderness to be tempted by the devil. After fasting for forty days and forty nights, he was hungry. The tempter came to him and said, "If you are the Son of God, tell these stones to become bread." Jesus answered, "It is written: 'Man shall not live on bread alone, but on every word that comes from the mouth of God.'" Then the devil took him to the holy city and had him stand on the highest point of the temple. "If you are the Son of God," he said, "throw yourself down. For it is written: 'He will command his angels concerning you, and they will lift you up in their hands so that you will not strike your foot against a stone.'" Jesus answered him, "It is also written: 'Do not put the Lord your God to the test.'*

Satan is very smart. He tried tempting Jesus in different ways, but how did Jesus respond? Jesus responds by saying, "*It is written.*" That's the key. What happens is that we need the Word of God to make things right, to walk right, and to understand what God wants. We need Hebrews 4:12, which says the Word is alive. Psalm 19:7 says it revives our soul. We need God's words in us. And the devil knows that, so he tries to distort the word, change it up, or use it out of context. Satan quoted the passage correctly, but only in one section. He didn't quote the rest of it correctly. Jesus brings it back into balance when He says to him, "***It is also written*** *do not put the Lord your God to the test.*" The devil only wants you to look at one side of things. He wants you to focus on one area of a passage so that he can warp the word and deceive you.

Do you know how much you need to know about the Word? All of it. If God wrote it and took the time to preserve it, you need to read it. Some parts are boring to our limited minds. I understand .... but get over it.

Sometimes, you might think, "Well, you don't understand Dave; that is 15 minutes out of my life." No, *you* don't understand. That could be 15 minutes where God hits you with the truth you absolutely need to hear. Just do it. Put down the other books you can't stop reading. Stop mindlessly flipping through the cable channels. You need to know all of the words, not just some of them. You need to have the Word permeating through your life and to get there; you need to be reading the Word every day.

Do you need to read for a certain amount of time every day? No. Do you need to read it in the morning as opposed to the evening? No. I don't care when you read it. Just read it. Does it have to be King James? Only if you are in England. Could it be the NIV? Yes. What about the Good News Bible? It worked for me. I got saved reading that version. Does any of that stuff matter, though? No. What matters is that you are in the Word and that you are in the Word all the time.

Why is that so important? I want to tell you why it is so important: ***it is for you***. God wants us in the Word for our own good. Why? Look at John 8:32:

> *Then you will know the truth, and the truth will set you free.*

In John 17:17, Jesus said, "*Father, sanctify them in thy truth; thy Word is truth.*" The Word of God is the truth. If you know the word—which is the truth—you will be set free. Why is that important? Well, if you are not set free, you are in bondage. Do you want to be in bondage? Do you like having these things in your life that are sucking away every moment of happiness? It's God's truth that sets you free from all of those things that pull you down.

Let me give you the final connection. This is really going to hit you. Look at John 8:44:

> *You belong to your father, the devil, and you want to fulfill your father's desires. He was a murderer from the beginning, not holding to the truth, for there is no truth in him. He speaks his native language when he lies, for he is a liar and the father of lies.*

Do you know that every one of the lies in your life comes from Satan? Every single one. Why? Because Satan is the father of lies. **And the only thing that defeats a lie is the truth**.

Here are some of the lies we tell ourselves. **I am not worthy enough to be a Christian. I have to work my way into heaven. God doesn't ever really hear me. I've blown it, and I can never recover.** Every single one of those lies needs to be blasted with the truth. What is the truth?

Remember Peter? Peter denied Jesus three times in a short period of time. Yet he turned out to be the apostle to the Jews, helped establish the church, and wrote two epistles in the Bible. He mentored Mark, who ended up writing a gospel. That is what happens when you make a big mistake and come to God. He forgives you, restores you, and redeems you.

1 John 3:1-2 says that we are the children of God. Yet some people still say, "No, I am a slug. I am worthless." No, you are a child of God. **God considers your value to be the price of the blood of Jesus**. How much is the blood of Christ worth? More than we can ever imagine. That is our value. That is the truth.

The whole point of you being in the Word is not for God to have a whole bunch of robotic people just going through the motions. He wants you to know the truth so you can be free from all the things that hurt you. He has given you the pathway in His Word. But, of course, the devil will do everything in his power to keep you from this book. He doesn't want you knowing it because when you know it, you're able to shut him down. You're able to put him out of business in your own life.

The foundation of your faith is the Word of God. Therefore, we need to constantly be in the Word so that we can be free and build the church together. Can I get an amen?

2

The Foundation of Our Faith, Part 2

When Jesus was baptized, the Father said, *"This is my Son in whom I am well pleased."* Well, all Jesus had done, at that point, was drown His head in the water. Nevertheless, the Father was pleased with Jesus's relationship with the Father and how that communion worked. The reality is that the <u>right relationship leads to the right ministry</u>, **and the right relationship is at the core of everything that true Christianity is**.

I am not talking about religion. Religions are going to come and go until the Lord comes back. All of that doesn't matter. What matters is doing the Christian life the way God wants us to do it. After 40 years of ministry, I am still convinced that there is no better way to do that than in your relationship with God. Everything flows out of our relationship with God, and every good thing comes out of it.

The reason man was created and put in the garden was so that God could come down in the cool of the day and spend time with Adam and Eve. And what was that all about? Well, it wasn't about God giving landscaping lessons. **It was about relationships and fellowship**. It was about hanging out together. And what Jesus did was restore what was lost in the Garden of Eden after the fall.

What is the basis of any relationship? Communication. Communication is manifested in two ways: talking and listening. The way you get to know somebody is to communicate with them. As you talk with someone and listen to them, and they do the same with you, you begin to get a feel for who they are, and vice versa. As you do that, you are building a relationship.

Well, it is no different between you and almighty God. In the previous chapter, we talked about how God talks to us through His Word. That is His part of the communication in our relationship with Him. In this chapter, we are going to talk about our part: **prayer**.

Prayer is absolutely essential for the believer. Some people have said that prayer is the "heartbeat of Christianity." That is an amazing saying. It doesn't matter where you are in the universe; nobody can stop you from praying to God and having communion with Him. No matter what situation we are in or where we are, nothing can stop our communion with God, period.

I want to tell you a story about a man. His name was Jonah. Jonah was a prophet of God. And God told Jonah that He wanted Jonah to go to Nineveh, and He wanted him to go to Nineveh to teach the Ninevites that they were sinning against God. God wanted them to hear a proclamation from a prophet so that they would repent. So, God said, "Jonah, go to Nineveh." Jonah thought, "Hmm. I don't really want to go to Nineveh. I think I will go down to Joppa and try to get to Tarshish because I don't really want to go to Nineveh."

Let me explain to you the geographical sequence that is taking place so you understand. Imagine that Jonah is in Los Angeles, and God says to Jonah, "Go to San Francisco."

Then Jonah says, "I think I'll make my way to San Diego." That's what's happening in Jonah's story. Tarshish is in the exact opposite direction of Nineveh.

Jonah hears God's command but decides, "Nah, I am not going to do that. I am going my way. I am going in this direction." When he gets to

Joppa, he finds a ship, and the ship is going to Tarshish. He was probably thinking, "Oh, yeah. I am on my way. I am out of here. I don't have to deal with anything." He thinks everything is going to be just fine.

He is on the boat when, all of a sudden, a big wind comes, causing enormous waves to swell up, and everybody in the boat is freaking out. The sailors are running around like crazy. And where is Jonah at this point? He is sleeping. He's completely out of it. He is sleeping in the boat while the boat is going down. The sailors begin to scream at him, "What are you doing? Get up! You know we are going down? Let's cast lots. Let's see whose fault this is." So, they roll the dice, and it turns out that it is Jonah's fault.

The sailors ask Jonah, "Who are you? What is going on here?"

Jonah replies, "Oh, *I am a servant of the most high God, who is also the God of the seas.*"

The sailors start to panic because they know that Jonah's God is not happy.

Jonah says to them, "I am going in the wrong direction. *You have got to throw me in the water.* It is the only way to calm the seas."

The sailors don't like that idea at all and reply, "Well, we are not going to throw you in the water."

The Bible says that they rowed harder, trying to get through the storm. But all their attempts were futile. In the end, they say, "*We don't want to be guilty of the blood of this man.*" So, they take Jonah. They threw him out of the boat and into the water. The storm stops. The sailors who threw him out of the water were not believers in Yahweh at that point. But they instantly became believers in Yahweh and began sacrificing and making vows to Him. Why? Because they were just in the middle of this horrendous storm. Then they threw Jonah out, and all of a sudden, the storm stopped. They start thinking, "We have been messing around with the wrong gods. This is the true God."

Jonah was in the water, just bobbing up and down. And a large fish comes and swallows Jonah. Jonah 2:1 says:

> *Then Jonah prayed to the Lord, his God, from the fish's belly.*

Here is how Jonah's brilliant plan has played out so far. **A)** He goes in the exact opposite direction from God. **B)** He finds a ship and assumes that everything is going fine. He thinks he's really going to get away with this. But he is bobbing up and down in the water. **D)** He now realizes things are going from bad to worse. So now, after all this takes place, what does Jonah do? Jonah prays, being the genius that he is.

When I get to heaven, this is what I'm going to ask Jonah: When you went on the boat, and you realized that the boat was about to break apart because of the storm, and you knew it was your fault, did you consider praying then?

And when they took you and threw you overboard, and your head hit the water, did you consider praying then?

And when the fish started to swallow you, either from your head first or your legs first, was that when you thought it was time to pray?

Or, better yet, was it after you were inside the belly of a fish for a day or three that you decided you needed to pray?

Was it a whale or a fish? It doesn't matter. He was compressed and swallowed by a fish, and it took him three days to figure out that he needed to pray. So, here's the big question: **When we are in trouble, what should we do?** James 5:13 says this:

Is anyone among you suffering? Let him pray.

We often pray last—not first—because we are lunatics. We are foolish. As soon as Jonah hit the water, he should have said, "I am sorry, Lord. This was dumb." When the fish started swallowing him, that was the time to tell God, "I really blew this. This was a bad call. Going in the opposite direction. I am sorry."

Sometimes, though, there is so much arrogance, so much pride, and so much stupidity in our lives that we just do every other possible thing in the universe first, and then we pray. It becomes our last resort.

Let's talk about prayer. Prayer is to ask. It is a request. It is to desire. It is to communicate. Here is the best definition of prayer you will ever hear: **talk to God**. You can pray in any way, shape, or form. It doesn't matter.

What the church has done is add on so many requirements for prayer. One of the great requirements involves your body parts doing certain things. The most common example of this is that when you pray, you must close your eyes. My extended family used to do this exercise when we would all be praying over a meal. While we were praying, we would all take a peek because we wanted to see who had their eyes open while they were praying. Inevitably, it was all of us because we were all looking to see who had their eyes open. But what does the Bible say? Jesus **lifted up his eyes** to heaven and prayed.

So, do you have to have your eyes closed when you pray? No. Do you have to have them open when you pray? No. Can you have one eye open and one eye closed? I feel like that is how most people drive these days. But the bottom line is that there are none of these kinds of body movement requirements. It doesn't matter if your hands are up or your hands are down. There is no requirement for body language during prayer.

The church has also given people certain requirements on the location of prayer. For example, some say you can only pray at church. Seriously, that is a requirement I've come across before. But it's totally unbiblical and totally impractical. We are able to pray all over the place, anywhere we are.

Some people think that when you pray, you have to say the words out loud. But is that true? Nehemiah didn't say a single word when he lifted up his prayer before the Lord because he was standing right next to the king. The king would have had his head cut off if he had said his prayer out loud while serving royalty. So, instead of speaking out loud, he just prayed silently, "Lord, be with me in this situation." Then he said, "Ok, king, here is what is going on." God answered that prayer.

Hannah also prayed in her heart. She moved her lips but didn't make a sound as she prayed. Eli saw that, and she thought she was drunk. So, does prayer have to be said out loud? No, it doesn't. But don't we often think in our minds, "Oh, God help me?" That is a prayer. That is communing.

That is talking to God, and there is nothing wrong with any of that.

You might be thinking, well, don't we have to pray in Jesus' name? No, we don't. **I don't know why you wouldn't pray in Jesus' name since He is worthy of all things and all authority in heaven and earth is under His name, and you come making requests in His name**. It is the greatest of all names. So why wouldn't you? But do you have to? No. Should you? Yes.

Can you see the insanity of these thought processes? We are constantly trying to meet all these religious rules and requirements. But it's much simpler than we make it sometimes. God hears us. He will listen to his people. He will help his people. Prayer is not a system of do's and don'ts. Prayer is about talking to God. And God will listen. Do you know there are many people who have prayed?

"I don't know which person is real: Jesus, Buddha, Allah, or Gandhi? But God, show me. I want to know." God has answered those prayers and led those people to a decision for Christ. Was that person a sinner at the time of the prayer? You bet. Did they pray in Jesus' name? No, but God still listened to them. Prayer works if you talk to God. He will lead you to the right place and guide you.

Don't get caught up in the legalistic arguments about how things should or shouldn't be done. It only causes more separation from God when the whole point of prayer is communion with Him.

But here is the key question: When we pray, do we expect an answer? My honest answer to you is, most of the time, **no**. You're probably thinking, "How can he say that?" Trust me, I am in good company on this one.

Let's look at Acts 12:1-14:

> *At about that time, Herod the King stretched out his hand to harass some in the church. Then he killed James, the brother of John, with the sword. And because he saw that it pleased the Jews, he proceeded further to seize Peter as well. Now it was during the Days of Unleavened Bread. So, when he had arrested*

him, he put him in prison and delivered him to four squads of soldiers to keep him, intending to bring him before the people after Passover.

Peter was therefore kept in prison, but constant prayer was offered to God for him by the church. And when Herod was about to bring him out, that night Peter was sleeping, bound with two chains between two soldiers, and the guards before the door were keeping the prison. Now behold, an angel of the Lord stood by him, and a light shone in the prison; and he struck Peter on the side and raised him up, saying, "Arise quickly!" And his chains fell off his hands.

Then the angel said to him, "Gird yourself and tie on your sandals"; and so he did. And he said to him, "Put on your garment and follow me." So, he went out and followed him. He did not know that what was done by the angel was real, but he thought he was seeing a vision. So, when they were past the first and second guard posts, they came to the iron gate that leads to the city, which opened to them of its own accord. So, they went out and went down one street, and immediately the angel departed from him.

And when Peter had come to himself, he said, "Now I know for certain that the Lord has sent His angel and has delivered me from the hand of Herod and from all the expectation of the Jewish people."

So, when he had considered this, he came to the house of Mary, the mother of John, whose surname was Mark, where many were gathered together praying. And as Peter knocked at the door of the gate, a girl named Rhoda came to answer. When she recognized Peter's voice, she did not open the gate because of her gladness but ran in and announced that Peter stood before the gate. But they said to her, "You are beside yourself!" Yet she kept insisting that it was so. So they said, "It is his angel."

So here are the members of the church praying for Peter's deliverance. Peter comes knocking on the door, and Rhoda goes to see who's there. It's Peter. So she runs back and tells the people praying that it is Peter. "You are nuts," they say. "You are out of your mind. You have lost it. What are you talking about?" They are arguing with her over whether it is Peter or not.

Why don't they believe Peter is at the door? Because that would be like, what? An answer to prayer. They were praying that he would be delivered. Then he gets delivered. But they don't even think it is possible.

When we pray, sometimes we pray out of ceremony. When we pray like that, it is a halfhearted, nonbelieving, and uncommitted prayer. The truth of the matter is that we don't believe that God is going to respond when we lift up that prayer. And you are not alone, because this is what these early church believers did. They just didn't believe that God would say yes and answer the prayer like that. Honestly, it's a bit of a funny story. Well, I guess if you were Peter, it wouldn't be that funny. Eventually, they let him in, though.

But the point is that there are these people praying for something to happen. God sends them the answer, and they are not even expecting God to come through. They don't believe that what they're praying for can actually happen.

Look at Mark 11:20-24:

> *In the morning, as they went along, they saw the fig tree wither from the roots. Peter remembered and said to Jesus, "Rabbi, look! The fig tree you cursed has withered!"*
>
> *"Have faith in God," Jesus answered. "Truly, I tell you, if anyone says to this mountain, 'Go, throw yourself into the sea,' and does not doubt*

> *in their heart but believes that what they say will happen, it will be done for them. Therefore, I tell you, whatever you ask for in prayer, believe that you have received it, and it will be yours.*

Did you catch that? **Believe that you have received it, and it will be yours**. There is a difference between believing <u>in</u> <u>the</u> Lord and "believing <u>the</u> Lord." When you pray, you already believe in the Lord. That is why you are praying. But what are we supposed to be doing after we have prayed? Believe that the Lord will answer!

Let's conclude the chapter with a part about prayer that never gets talked about. It's found in John 14:12-14:

> Very truly, I tell you, whoever believes in me will do the works I have been doing, and they will do even greater things than these because I am going to the Father. And I will do whatever you ask in my name, so that the Father may be glorified in the Son. Therefore, you may ask me for anything in my name, and I will do it.

If you are looking for a reason to pray, here it is: **answered prayer glorifies God**. That is the reason to pray. Yes, it does give you peace. Yes, it does give you joy. Yes, it does bring you closer to God. Yes, it will rescue you. But above all, <u>answered</u>

prayer glorifies God. And that should be reason enough for us to pray anywhere, anytime, and anyhow.

27

3

The Highest Calling

2 Timothy 4:1-4 says this:

> *"In the presence of God and of Christ Jesus, who will judge the living and the dead, and in view of his appearing and his kingdom, I give you this charge: Preach the word; be prepared in season and out of season; correct, rebuke, and encourage—with great patience and careful instruction. The time will come when people will not put up with sound doctrine. Instead, to suit their own desires, they will gather around them a great number of teachers to say what their itching ears want to hear. They will turn their ears away from the truth and turn aside to myths."*

As Paul instructs Timothy in this passage, he tells him, "Hey, do you know what? There's going to be a time when people are not going to listen to sound doctrine." Sound doctrine is not going to remain relevant. What's going to become relevant is that people will want to hear **what they want to hear**. Because they've heard *this,* and they've heard *that,* they will pick and choose what they like. They're going to go to places where they can <u>feel good</u> and be told they're good. Everything's good. There are no issues. There are no problems.

In essence, Paul warns Timothy, who's taking over for Paul, that this <u>will</u> happen. This is not what *might* happen. It's definitely going to happen. **People are going to go to myths**. They're going to use myths as their sound doctrine and false things that are not true. Things that make everybody feel fluffy. You know, like nice little cotton candy balls.

We used to call it *greasy grace.* Cotton candy grace. Everything's just nice. It's all great. Oh, don't worry, it doesn't matter. "You go on being a mass murderer, no problems whatsoever. No questions, we all love you.". Paul sounds the warning bell. "No, no, no, it must be based on sound doctrine." It's sound doctrine, and that's what you have to stick with.

Where do we get sound doctrine?

Sound doctrine comes between Genesis 1:1 and Revelation 22:21. Sound doctrine does not take one portion of the Bible and only concentrates on that one portion of the Bible. Sound doctrine uses the whole Bible. Teaches the whole Bible. Believes in the whole Bible. Trusts the Holy Spirit for the whole Bible.

God created the universe; he can write a BOOK.

I want to talk to you about something that will happen to you or is happening to you but will probably happen again. I want to talk to you about what you are going to encounter if you are a sincere servant of Jesus Christ. If you are an authentic servant of Jesus Christ, I want to tell you about two things that are going to take place for you. And these will happen because you believe in the truth of the Bible and seek to obey the sound doctrine in the Bible. No sugar coating.

I can absolutely promise you that God will put you through seminaries. The first seminary is called **_being yielded_**. The second seminary He will put you through is called **_being broken_**. According to the whole of Scripture, I want to promise you that God will make you look more like Jesus in your Christian walk than you do right now. There will be yielding on your part in this process, and there will also be breaking on your part.

Let's turn to Genesis, chapter 22. We'll start with verse 1.

"Sometime later, God tested Abraham. He said to him, 'Abraham!' 'Here I am,' he replied. Then God said, 'Take your son, your only son, whom you love— Isaac—and go to the region of Moriah. Sacrifice him there as a burnt offering on a mountain I will show you.' So, early the next morning, Abraham got up and loaded his donkey. He took with him two of his servants and his son Isaac.

When he had cut enough wood for the burnt offering, he set out for the place God had told him about. On the third day, Abraham looked up and saw the place in the distance. He said to his servants, 'Stay here with the donkey while the boy and I go over there. First, we will worship, and then we will come back to you.'

Abraham took the wood for the burnt offering and placed it on his son Isaac, and he himself carried the fire and the knife. And the two of them went up together; Isaac spoke up and said to his father Abraham, 'Father?' 'Yes, my son?' Abraham replied. 'The fire and wood are here,' Isaac said, 'but where is the lamb for? the burnt offering?' Abraham answered, 'God himself will provide the lamb for the burnt offering, my son.' And the two of them went on together.

When they reached the place God had told him about, Abraham built an altar there and arranged the wood on it. He bound his son Isaac and laid him on the altar, on top of the wood. Then he reached out his hand and took the knife to slay his son. But the angel of the Lord called out to him from heaven, 'Abraham! Abraham!' 'Here I am,' he replied. 'Do not lay a hand on the boy,' he said. 'Do not do anything to him. Now I know that you fear God because you have not withheld from me your son, your only son.'"

I think it's easy to read this story and just skip right by what took place. We just think, "Oh, okay. Well, he didn't... Nothing happened. No big deal." The only description we're getting from God in lieu of Abraham and Isaac is a short description in verse 2. First, God tells us he's going to test Abraham. Then He says, "Take your son, Abraham, whom you love." There's an indication in Hebrew that this was a very passionate and deep love.

Why wouldn't it be? This is a son to a father, a child born out of the promise of God. **This child represents the promises made by God to Abraham**. I mean, Abraham was wandering out in the desert, trying to find his way, trying to follow the Lord. The Lord promised him a nation out of his loins, and this child was that promise. God said, "I want you to go up, and I want you to make a sacrifice." So, as Abraham is walking with his son, verse 5 says that he looked up and saw the place from a distance.

If you're a parent, I want you to take that moment to know what is supposed to occur. You look up and see the place. You know what is about to take place, how that makes you feel. Then you go a little further, and you have to leave the servants. You take the wood, and you put it on your kid... *Abraham puts it on his son.* His son carries his own execution materials, heading up the hill, while Abraham has the knife and the fire.

Abraham knows exactly what he's going to do because God told him what he's got to do. Then he gets up there, and instead of Abraham pleading with God (which I mean, I think I would've. I would have said, "Well, now let's talk about this." Do you know what I mean? I would have some moments there), he starts building an altar. He grabs Isaac. He ties him up and gets ready to chop him. Some theologians have said that God would never have let Abraham do it. That's not the point.

The point is that Abraham tied him up, put him on there, and was ready to chop him. You think, "Why?" I mean, that's brutal. That's awful. That's terrible. Today, we'd be calling the FBI and having a whole show on it, but this is a story that stands the test of time. Well, for Judeo and Christian people, the reason that God asked (forced, commanded) Abraham to take Isaac up and put him on the altar was this single reason alone. It's hard for me to say. It's hard for me to hear. I imagine it's hard for you to hear, **but no other gods are allowed regarding God**. There is nothing that can gather our hearts and be so clouded in our hearts, even our own children, that we can put it in any esteem near God. If we do, God will make us cut it out. You think, "But I'm a father. That's brutal." That's what God demands. There are no other gods. There are no other shrines. Nothing else was before him.

Idolatry is putting anything before God. Like me, do you know that we commit a form of idolatry when we worry about our situation and don't believe in God? Why? We believe the situation is greater than God. We give more power and more worship time to the problem than to God. That's idolatry. Not allowed. Forbidden. Anything in our lives that stands between God and us is our new god, and God doesn't want it there. And no matter what or who it is, He will not let that stay there.

So God's answer is, "Cut it out. Get rid of it. <u>Before</u> <u>I make you kill it, you'd better get rid of it.</u>" I don't care how serious it is—a relationship, fears, anxiety, worship, or a misunderstanding. It doesn't matter to me. It's between you and God.

Whatever it is, it's got to go.

Here's you. Here's God. If there's anything in between, get rid of it. I don't care what it is because if you don't, God, at some point, is going to call you on the table and tell you to get rid of it. You say, "Well, how do you know that, David? I mean, this was Abraham."

Okay. Galatians, chapter 3, verse 29:

> *"If you belong to Christ, then you are Abraham's seed and heirs according to the promise."*

If you're a Christian, you're connected to Abraham. Look what God did to Abraham. There's your connection. If you're a Christian and you belong to Jesus, then you're connected to Abraham. Abraham was required to have no other shrines. There are no other gods. Nothing stands between them. God is a jealous God.

I know we all struggle with sin, issues, and different things that go on in life. I'm not telling you you're not going to struggle. You're going to go through tough times and have tougher times. I'm just telling you that it always comes down to you and God. You're in that prayer closet. **There better be nothing that stands between you and God**. Period! Or you could be looking at a sacrifice that you don't want to make. So, make it <u>now</u> before God makes you do it. Does everybody understand that?

All he is saying is that we love God. "First, love the Lord God with all your heart, soul, strength, and mind." All that matters is obeying the first commandment. That's a tough seminary. Do you know how many times I've had to sacrifice and do that spiritually in my mind and reestablish and make sure God had first place? I've done it a thousand times. I can imagine you guys have done that, too. It's still continually required. God is a jealous God. He doesn't like competition. That is seminary number one. If you can learn that, you just did two years of academic seminary, for real.

Here's the next seminary. This one might not be as harsh, but on the other hand, this one's worse. Luke, chapter 20. This will tweak your brain. This is the new slant on this particular old verse. Luke, chapter 20, verse 17 says,

> *"Jesus looked directly at them and asked, 'Then what is the meaning of that which is written: "The stone the builders rejected has become the cornerstone"? Everyone who falls on that stone will be broken to pieces; anyone on whom it will fall will be crushed.'"*

You have two different kinds of people here. One group of people falls on the stone, and they are broken to pieces. The stone falls on the other people, and they are crushed (as in bye-bye). The first seminary I talked to you about was being yielded. Having no other gods and no other shrines. That's just solid… It's a given.

Everybody understands that, but the second one's a little tougher. It has to do with being broken. *What does being broken* mean? *Broke* as in broke in dollars? Well, we're all living that half the time. That doesn't matter. No, being broken is much deeper than that. Let me explain brokenness.

Psalm 31, verse 12, written by King David.

> *"I am forgotten as though I were dead; I have become like broken pottery."*

Did everybody get that? Now go to Romans, chapter 9, verse 20.

"But who are you, a human being, to talk back to God? 'Shall what is formed say to the one who formed it, "Why did you make me like this?"' Does not the potter have the right to make out of the same lump of clay some pottery for special purposes and some for common use?"

Let me tell you about the second seminary, called Brokenness.

There was this young lad. He kills this giant. He's the bomb. Everybody loves him. They're singing songs about him for crying out loud. Everybody adores this guy. Before this, Samuel comes, and he takes a flask of oil and puts it over his head. He says, "David, you're going to be the king. You're going to be defined as a man after God's heart. You're so blessed. But before you become king, we need you to enter into a little seminary." "What might that be?" You're going to find out, Davey. You're going to find out.

David's in the palace. The next thing you know, he's dodging a spear. He's dodging another spear. He must have been thinking, "What's going on here?" What he finds out is that his new school, his new seminary, from God Almighty is this class in brokenness. Because, on the way to being the king, God has David sleeping in caves, running for his life, and writing psalms of appeals, mercy, and grace. <u>For ten years</u>.

> *Psalm 23: "...though I walk through the valley of the shadow of death..."*

These psalms of faith will inspire him and strengthen him, but while he's going through the process of becoming king, **he's in this school of brokenness**. God is breaking him down. In essence, everything that Saul had, God is breaking out of David. Until David has no Saul left in him. It's beautiful imagery if you understand it. ***God was killing Saul out of David.***

It's brokenness so God can mold you, change you, and alter you. It's the willingness. It's Jesus in the garden saying, "Not my will be done." It's "Whatever you want. You are in charge." It's, "I will have no other god before me, and do you know what? I will now lay down my agenda and pick up yours."

It's called being yielded. It's called being broken. Yet, it is required of Christians. The reason it is required is because of where it will lead you. It leads you and me to the greatest place ever. Where it leads us is to the ultimate place, which is God's perfect will.

Hopefully, I will not discourage you and will lead you to the place where you can say, "This is where I want to be." So, here's a little foundational work from the two seminaries: being yielded and being broken. The purpose of graduating is for us to reach **the highest call**.

Philippians, chapter 3, verse 4:

> *"...though I have reasons for such confidence. If someone else thinks they have reasons to put confidence in the flesh, I have more: circumcised on the eighth day, of the people of Israel, of the tribe of Benjamin, a Hebrew of Hebrews; in regard to the law, a Pharisee; as for zeal, persecuting the church; as for righteousness based on the law, faultless."*

Oh, Paul did have an ego when he was writing that, didn't he? It's just a classic little line. These are his religious accomplishments that he is sharing with us. He's speaking from a human point of view. "I did *this*. I was a Pharisee. I was *this*. You know, I was born into *this* family. I was president of *this*. Senator to *this*. I was *this*. Look what I did." It's all his little accomplishments, right? And then he nails it down.

> *"But whatever were gains to me, I now consider loss for the sake of Christ. What is more, I consider everything a loss because of the surpassing worth of knowing Christ Jesus, my Lord, for whose sake I have lost all things. I consider them garbage that I may gain Christ and be found in him, not having a righteousness of my own that comes from the law, but that which is through faith in a Christ—the righteousness that comes from God on the basis of faith."*

<u>The highest call for any Christian is right there</u>.

How you get there is that you learn to be yielded, and you learn to be broken. You make sure there are no other gods before you. You make sure that there's nothing that you're not moldable in. You make sure that you're pliable Silly.

Put all the time for God to use you, and you live in verse 8, which is living in this understanding.

> *"What is more, I consider everything a loss because of the surpassing worth of knowing Christ Jesus my Lord...."*

Everything else doesn't matter. It just doesn't matter. Because everything else Paul says in the next verse is this:

"...for whose sake I have lost all things. I consider them garbage...."

Paul says, "I consider it rubbish. It's ridiculous. There is nothing more important to me than knowing Jesus. Everything else is irrelevant. Religious accomplishments mean nothing. **It's all about knowing Jesus**." It's not all about ***knowing*** Jesus, because in James, chapter 2, verse 19, the Bible says if you believe in God, you do well. The demons believe and shudder. Oh, they believe in God, per se, but they don't know him; they know **of** him.

Everything you have done in your life, that you are doing, and that you're going to do is absolute garbage compared to knowing Jesus. Period.

You think, "Well, that's a pretty bold statement. Are you trying to say that knowing Jesus is more important than ministry?" No, **I am not** going to say that. **Jesus is**.

Let's go to Luke, chapter 10. I don't have to say it. He said it.

In Luke, chapter 10, listen to the definition that Jesus gives us. It just makes everything else as clear as it could be. If you never do another thing in your life, listen to this. If you never hear another truth in your life. Hear this one. Paul said that everything else compared to knowing Jesus is rubbish. It's garbage. Listen to what Jesus says.

Luke, chapter 10, verse 38:

> *"As Jesus and his disciples were on their way, he came to a village where a woman named Martha opened her home to him. She had a sister called Mary, who sat at the Lord's feet listening to what he said."*

What was Mary doing? Sitting at the Lord's feet, right? She was sitting at the Lord's feet. What she's doing is pretty obvious, right? But Martha was distracted by all the preparations that had to be made.

> *"She came to him and asked, 'Lord, don't you care that my sister has left me to do the work by myself? Tell her to help me!'"*

"I'm busy working here, serving the Lord; I'm doing this by myself. So, tell my sister to quit being a lazy bum and come and help me." Verse 41:

> *"'Martha, Martha,' the Lord answered, 'you are worried and upset about many things, but few things are needed—or indeed only one. Mary has <u>chosen</u> what <u>is better</u>, and it will not be taken away from her.'"*

Does that need a commentary? I mean, she's just sitting there listening to what Jesus has to say, and all this other fuss and buss is going around her, and she's just sitting there. So Jesus defends her: "She's not going anywhere. She's right where she's supposed to be."

Because it's not a religion. I know we have often made it that way. So many others have made it that way, too. But that is not what it is supposed to be. This is about knowing Jesus. That's what this is.

We're not even on our home planet. We're even called *strangers* and *aliens* on this planet. We're not even there yet. So everything else, compared to knowing Jesus, doesn't matter.

Well, you might think, well, that's oversimplifying. Uh-huh. I think that was the whole intent. God wants you not to be so nervous about **everything else** that's going on and to remember what's really important. Him.

You may think we are supposed to occupy until He comes. Of course, we're going to do our best to do the best we can.

But it's not more important than continually knowing Jesus. Sorry.

In Philippians, chapter 1, verse 21, Paul says,

"...to live is Christ, and to die is gain."

Okay. What would you like to do with that? I mean, living is about Jesus, and dying is better because then you're closer to Jesus. **So, I guess this whole thing is about Jesus.** Go figure.

That's the whole point. It's all about Jesus. Stop. Don't sweat the small stuff. Yeah, I know you've got a lot of stuff to do, and you've got a lot of hurts to work through. You want to do *this* for business. You want *that* in a relationship. Yep, yep, yep, yep, yep, yep, yep, yep, yep. I had a Jewish mother; I've heard it all. Okay? You're not going to tell me something I haven't heard along those lines, trust me.

It's not more important than just knowing Jesus.

I told you all that stuff just to get you to this point. But, listen, no other gods, be broken, all for this understanding, that we may know Him.

That's all he wants. Revelation, chapter 3, verse 20:

"Behold, I stand at the door and knock...."

Irony. Jesus didn't say that to non-Christians. He wrote it to a church.

"...I stand at the door and knock...." "Let me in."

It is the cornerstone of everything that is Christian. Jesus says, "You search the scriptures because in them you think they have life; these are what's testifying of me."

It's all religious *this* or all religious *that.* Stop it. It's not.

It's a relationship.

It's not a religion. Go talk to him. "Well, I want Him to talk back to me." It's called the Bible. Try it. You may hear something. I guess that's why it's called "the Word of God."

There you go. I mean, there it is. Enjoy it. Live it.

Breathe it.

Everything else is rubbish.

4

Sorry God

If I'm going to title this chapter, which technically I need to do, the title will be *Sorry, God*. Ephesians 4:30:

> *"And do not grieve the Holy Spirit of God, with whom you were sealed for the day of redemption."*

The passage is not too complex. Several of you have read it many, many times before. The word *grieved* is not the same as the word *quenched* in Thessalonians. *Grieved* is a Greek word that means to make sad.

The statement that God is making to His people is, "Don't make the Holy Spirit sad." In a Bible study, we were discussing the Trinity. Listen. This is not "Candyland 101." This is Christianity, and that's what we're talking about. There's a Trinity, and it's the Father, the Son, and the Holy Spirit. It's three in one and one in three. All three are there. All three are equal. All three are part of the process.

There's something called the *ordo salutis,* which is not something you'll ever use for the rest of your life. It means the order (or the process) of salvation.

There is also a process within the Godhead, and it has to do with the following: The Son doesn't send the Father, but the Father sends the Son, and the Son sends the Spirit. The Spirit does not send the Son. But the Spirit led the Son during the incarnation (When Jesus [God] became a human).

What I think has happened in the universal church today is that we have become an overly culture-oriented group. We are so image-focused that it's not too difficult for the church to acknowledge God the Father. People understand the concept of a father. It's not that difficult to understand God the Son, who's supposed to be the Savior. That's kind of "Okay." Somebody is saving the day. Similar to somebody hitting a home run at the last minute. That's saving the day. We get that.

But God the Spirit... that's a different story. The church has a very tight, restrictive mentality when it comes to the Holy Spirit. Do you want to know why? Because we don't get the Holy Spirit the same way, we can get God the Father or God the Son. Because we don't get it, we're like, "Eh, let's not go too far into talking about this. We don't know much about the Holy Spirit."

Well, we do know a lot about the Holy Spirit. We know He is God. We know Peter referred to Him as God in Acts, chapter 5, when Ananias and Sapphira were told that they lied to the Holy Spirit, and then in the very next breath, Peter goes, "You didn't lie to men; you lied to God," calling the Holy Spirit God. So we know he's God. When we sing "Holy, Holy, Holy," the famous hymn, we're singing to the Father, the Son, and the Holy Spirit. Nobody has any arguments with that.

But I'm telling you that there is a special position regarding the Holy Spirit because only the Holy Spirit gets this little tag: "If you blaspheme the Holy Spirit, you will never be forgiven, not in this life or the next." Amazingly, Jesus said that. He didn't say that about the Father, and He didn't say that about himself.

What's going on? What's the deal there? So the Triune God knows that men would belittle the work of the Spirit, and the Spirit Himself (being God) wanted us to be aware of that. As Christians, that is not the way we should treat God.

The Holy Spirit is an active part of our existence, but you may be similar to me... I think I have grieved the Holy Spirit on more than one occasion. I have definitely quenched the Holy Spirit on a regular basis, but I've also grieved him. I've made him sad. I think I've done things and said things (and thought things) that the Holy Spirit was not appreciative of. "That's impressive, Dave. Way to think those wrong thoughts." I know the Holy Spirit was declaring, "That's not good. Don't do that." Every one of us has had that happen to us.

Quite frankly, as mature Christians, we should all **be sorry** for the things we've done that have made the Holy Spirit sad. But I don't know if you ever feel like you've done that. If you haven't, you've only been a Christian for probably about 10 minutes because the reality is that in your Christian walk, you do the wrong things. Sometimes, bad things happen.

Have you ever thought to yourself or said to yourself, "I shouldn't do that? That's bad. That's dumb." Afterward, you're hitting yourself in the head.

So, I just want to review the reality that we've made the Holy Spirit sad. Then, I want to talk about what the Holy Spirit has done for us and what we need to do to flip that around. I want to show you how important the Holy Spirit is in the whole process of our Christian walk. I want to show you that the Holy Spirit is involved in our spiritual birth process.

Luke 1:21-34:

> *"In the sixth month, God sent the angel Gabriel to Nazareth, a town in Galilee, to a virgin pledged to be married to a man named Joseph, a descendant of David. The virgin's name was Mary. The angel went to her and said, 'Greetings, you who are highly favored! The Lord is with you.' Mary was greatly troubled by his words and wondered what kind of greeting this might be.*
>
> *But the angel said to her, 'Do not be afraid, Mary; you have found favor with God. You will be with a child and give birth to a son, and you are to give him the name Jesus. He will be great and will be called the Son of the Most High. The Lord God will give him the throne of his father David, and he will reign over the house of Jacob forever; his kingdom will never end.' 'How will this be,' Mary asked the angel, 'since I am a virgin?'"*

What Mary said was, "How are you going to do that? I'm a virgin." She was kind of curious as to the methodology that was taking place, so she goes, "How will this be? I don't get it." Not that she doubted; she was curious.

Some people get confused between Zechariah and Mary. They think Zechariah asked the same question as Mary did when he heard the angel's announcement regarding his wife Elizabeth getting pregnant. However, it was not the same question. What Zechariah said was, "How do I know you're for real?"

Back to Mary. Luke 1:35-37:

> *"The angel answered, 'The Holy Spirit will come upon you, and the power of the Most High will overshadow you. So the holy one to be born will be called the Son of God. Even Elizabeth, your relative, will have a child in her old age, and she, who was said to be barren, is in her sixth month. For nothing is impossible with God.'"*

Let me explain to you how profound this statement is. We talk about it at Christmas, and we have a little pageant, a little play, a little nativity scene, and we say, "Ooh, that's so nice." The Holy Spirit of God, the essence, power, personality, and most intimate element of God Himself moved into a virgin woman and created life. That life is Jesus Christ. Every time you think of Jesus, you must understand that His birth and existence literally transpired through the exacting and moving of the Holy Spirit of God. Jesus was born by the Holy Spirit. Do we understand how important that is? You have to wrap your mind around it. "Wait a minute." He is a man (the Mary part) and God (the Holy Spirit part). He was a man and a god. He's the only one who could represent God to man and man to God (*one Mediator*). He's the only one qualified because he has both natures in him. He has both human nature and divine nature. He's the only one who could bring the two together. That's the whole point. But He's born of the Holy Spirit, as are we.

Titus 3:3 states,

> *"At one time, we too were foolish, disobedient, deceived, and enslaved by all kinds of passions and pleasures. We lived in malice and envy, being hated and hating one another. But when the kindness and love of God Savior appeared; he saved us, not because of the righteous things we had done, but because of his mercy. He saved us through the washing of rebirth and renewal by the Holy Spirit...."*

You are born again by the Spirit of God. How important is that? If you <u>ain't</u> born again, you <u>ain't</u> getting in. That's pretty important. It's significant to understand that the Holy Spirit was crucial in the birth of Jesus Christ, and the Holy Spirit is crucial in **your** rebirth.

Now, it comes through the justification of Jesus Christ. **Everything does**. But the Holy Spirit has an active role in your becoming a Christian. Without the Holy Spirit, you're not getting in. <u>It's just that simple</u>.

"Oh, those born-agains...." Yeah. We born-agains are the ones who are going in. Sorry. I can't help that. That's not my fault (John 3:3).

Not only is the Holy Spirit involved in our spiritual birthing, but He's also involved in the start of our ministries. Did you know that God didn't save you so that you could go to church? Your ministry is not to sit on your blessed assurance and go to church. That's not what the ministry is. That's not the purpose. Ministry means service. Does everybody get that? The point of ministry is to serve others, love others the way Christ commands, and reflect Jesus in everything.

So, you have a ministry. Everybody reading this has a ministry. It might be the simplest thing. It might be passing out bulletins. It might be picking up or cleaning chairs at the end of the service (which somebody has to do). It might be any of those things, but what I'm telling you is that you need to recognize that you have a ministry, a purpose, and a call from God, and the Holy Spirit is crucial in that process.

Look at Luke, chapter 4. This is the beginning of Jesus' ministry. This is how Jesus started **His** ministry, faced the enemy, and did what *He* had to do.

> *"Jesus, full of the Holy Spirit, returned from the Jordan and was led by the Spirit in the desert...."*

The Spirit of God filled up Jesus Christ so **He could finish His mission of saving us**. But, first, He used the power of the Holy Spirit to help those around Him.

Another text is Matthew 3:13:

> *"Then Jesus came from Galilee to Jordan to be baptized by John. But John tried to deter him, saying, 'I need to be baptized by you, and do you come to me?' Jesus replied, 'Let it be so now; it is proper for us to do this to fulfill all righteousness.' Then John consented. As soon as Jesus was baptized, he went up out of the water. At that moment, heaven was opened,*

> *and he saw the Spirit of God descending like a dove and lighting on him. And a voice from heaven said, 'This is my Son, whom I love; with him, I am well pleased.'"*

The Holy Spirit is not only involved in our salvation process to get us saved; the Holy Spirit is necessary for our life to get our ministry rolling, whatever that ministry is. I don't care if it *is* passing out bulletins. Or sweeping parking lots. We need the Holy Spirit to do this stuff with the right *servant* spirit. We can't do this righteous servant stuff in our strength. How strong do we think we are?

Here, I'll give you one. You tell me how you are doing in *this* one. <u>Love your enemy</u>. How do you do that?

I can't even love my friends, let alone my enemies. I can't even love *myself* the right way, let alone my enemies. Without the power of God and the Holy Spirit, it cannot be done. Then it's going to come to the things that are a little more fun. This is all coming down to a single point, as it often does.

The Holy Spirit is responsible for starting our lives, participating in the beginnings of our ministry, and empowering us to live like Jesus. I don't know about you, but in my life, from time to time (every three hours), I need help. I don't know. Maybe it's me, but I feel I need God to support me, guide me, direct me, and teach me. It's just one of those things I'm often thinking, "What am I doing?"

Here is John 16:12. This is a critical instruction from Jesus.

> *"I have much more to say to you, more than you can now bear. But when he, the Spirit of Truth, comes, he will guide you into all truth."*

Did you know the Holy Spirit is supposed to be your guide? Isn't that unbelievable? We talked about this before. The Holy Spirit is supposed to be your counselor. **How are your counseling sessions going**? He's your comforter. **How are your comforting sessions going**?

"Oh, man! We're in trouble here, aren't we?" Well, a little bit.

Here, the Holy Spirit is supposed to guide us. Hey, do you need guidance in life? The B-I-B-L-E tells you what you must know. The Holy Spirit wrote the Bible. Jesus says the Holy Spirit will guide you into all truth.

Wow! I need help with that. Is it just me? I need to spend time with the Holy Spirit. The Bible says I'm supposed to fellowship with the Holy Spirit (2 Corinthians 13:14). **Am I supposed to <u>fellowship</u> with the Holy Spirit?** How is that going? Wow! I need help.

Again, this might be me. I'm sure this is me. There are times when I wake up in the morning and think, "I just don't know if I can do another day." I don't know if you guys have ever felt that way. You wake up sighing. Instead of getting up and going, "All right!" you get up and sigh. It's the same as you saying, "Okay. I'm going to force myself to get up." I know what that is. I'm feeling weak, and I'm feeling tired.

Ephesians 3:14:

> *"For this reason, I kneel before the Father, from whom his whole family in heaven and on earth derives its name. I pray that out of his glorious riches, he may strengthen you with power through his Spirit in your inner being...."*

Are you feeling weak? Are you feeling tired? Feeling run down? Well, guess what the Holy Spirit's job is to do? **To strengthen you and me internally**.

Do you ever feel like you need internal strength? Unfortunately, I cannot be the only person on this planet who needs that. I mean, there are times when I'm thinking, "Ugh!" That's when you get up and think, "Getting up and doing all of the things I'm supposed to do, **or** putting my head back down on the pillow and telling everybody I'm sick." Confess. Which one?

It's when you feel that way that you need strengthening from God. The part of God that's going to strengthen you in this is called the *Holy Spirit*. He's right there waiting for you to ask him to help you.

Did anybody ever go through the honeymoon period in Christianity? In the beginning, when you became a Christian, it was akin to, "Oh my gosh! I'm a Christian!" Right? You would pray, and you would pray *anything*, and God answered *everything*, and you were just rocking and rolling. You were thinking, "I'm in touch with the divine." You were walking around with that mentality.

You can pray a prayer, and it halfway dribbles out of your mouth in that honeymoon period. God still said yes. "There it is. All right!" I had a great season of the honeymoon period, and I could know, feel, and rejoice in the love of God because the love of God was everywhere. I was loved. Awesome! "I don't care *what* happens in the universe. I'm loved."

Then, after a little while, it seems as though you go through this period when the honeymoon is over. You know that fun feeling, the 'every prayer answered' experience, isn't happening quite the same. So then you're contemplating, "I don't feel the love of God the way I used to feel the love. I really wish I could feel the love of God again."

Then you start praying, and God doesn't say, "Yes." So now he starts saying, "**No**." Before, it wasn't the same.

The honeymoon period is over, and now you're into the *working it out* part of it, and you're going, "Uh Oh."

We all get to this space where you want to feel the love of God, just as you did in the very beginning when everything was on fire. Remember that? Do you guys know what I'm talking about? Check out Hebrews 10:32.

But here's a way to go to the bank, take out a loan, and buy a clue: Romans 5:5:

> *"And hope does not disappoint us because God has poured out his love into our hearts by the Holy Spirit, whom he has given us."*

Do you know why we've gotten away from that? It's because we're not sensitive to the Holy Spirit the way we used to be. We're making the Holy Spirit sad. We're not paying attention to or recognizing his position. And that love we felt in the beginning? This came from the Holy Spirit. That love is ours through the Holy Spirit.

<u>This is not to glorify feelings</u>. I repeat: **<u>This is not to glorify feelings</u>**. Feelings need to follow the truth. <u>Always</u>. But being Christians does not mean we have lost our loving feelings (Get it?).

Or we say *this* because we're dumb enough to buy into *this* one: "Well, now that God really knows me...." Now that he really knows you, huh? That's good. It's a good thing God is not omniscient. But, again, that love is ours through the Holy Spirit.

I'm coming right down to a single point. Two more, and then you'll get it. Romans 8:16:

> *"The Spirit himself testifies with our spirit that we are God's children."*

Does the devil ever come up to you and whisper, "If you are a Christian...?" "If you're really saved...." "If God really loves you..."? Just as he said to Jesus, "If thou be the Son of God...." Same thing. Same exact temptation. Same exact line. **Same exact lie**. Same one. No different.

Here, in Romans 8:16, the Bible tells us that the Holy Spirit assures us that we're His. "Ooh. What do you mean?" Well, I can read it again. I think I got that right.

"The Spirit himself testifies with our spirit that we are God's children." Yeah. I think that's right. The Holy Spirit testifies to that affirmation.

"I just want to know I'm going to make it. I just want to know I'm God's kid." Well, perhaps you should be listening to the Holy Spirit a tad bit more because that's one of the great places where you find that out.

Last and not least, by any means, is Luke 10:21.

> *"At that time Jesus, full of joy through the Holy Spirit...."*

Oh, man! The Holy Spirit guides me; He strengthens me; He loves me; He starts the ministry; He starts my birth; He assures me; *and He's responsible for joy in my heart.* Yep! That's it. *"Jesus, full of joy through the Holy Spirit...."*

Has that joy of yours been long lost to the left side of the lake somewhere? Well, guess what? If you have more of the Holy Spirit in you, you will have more joy in you. If you have more of the joy in you, you'll have more of the strength in you. That's the bottom line. You need to have the Holy Spirit active. **You need to have the Holy Spirit active in everything**.

I simply picked out a few principles. Do you know how many I could have pulled out of this? But we've spent a lot of time making the Holy Spirit sad. Not the best plan. So, here's the answer: stop doing that and do what is right. It's just one verse.

It's all you need to know. Ready?

Luke, chapter 11, verse 9:

> *"So I say to you: Ask, and it will be given to you; seek, and you will find; knock, and the door will be opened to you. For everyone who asks receives; he who seeks finds, and to him who knocks, the door will be opened. Which of you fathers, if your son asks for a fish, will give him a snake instead? Or if he asks for an egg, will you give him a scorpion? If you then, though you are evil, know how to give good gifts to your children, how much more will your Father in heaven give the Holy Spirit to those who ask him?"*

I do not believe I can make this any clearer than what I just said. I don't believe I can expound on this to make it any more obvious.

It's really simple. All of these things that we lack because we're not in communion with the Holy Spirit can be rectified in one moment by all of us going, "God, I need the Holy Spirit, please."

The Scripture is quite clear. If our children ask us for bread, do we give them scorpions? No.

God will give you the Holy Spirit if you...*wait for it...*

ask Him. Wow!

What a novel concept. He is going to be the same as a father who gives his child something he needs. Do you think, "Well, do I have to respond to this in a certain fashion? Do I have to speak in tongues, prophesy reminiscent of an Old Testament prophet, dance, sing, spin, twirl, preach a perfect 4-point homiletical message, or start talking with long-drawn-out sounds? Or do I have to bark in the same way as a dog? **None of that is here**.

Just ask Him *to cry out loud* (yeah, *that* crying out loud). He's more than capable of taking care of the answer. It's a simple matter of... Do we recognize that the Holy Spirit is at the beginning of our salvation? Does he stop? Check out Galatians 3:1-5.

He helps start your ministry; He guides you; He strengthens you; and He loves you. <u>Don't you feel that you would enjoy that love in your heart again?</u> He assures you. Isn't that assurance important? It's important to me. He gives us joy. Oh! I could use *that*.

The bottom line is that we *need* the Holy Spirit, and we can **have** the Holy Spirit, but it does take this big thing: **asking**. The Father wants us to ask, or it wouldn't be in the book. What's the point? We just must get this stuff on track. Do you want to bring more joy into your life? Do you want to have more peace? Do you want to have more grace? Well, get more of God in your life. It's all coming through the Holy Spirit.

As was wisely said in a Bible study not too long ago, the Holy Spirit is doing the job for Jesus that Jesus was doing when Jesus was on earth. Now, the Holy Spirit is doing it for Jesus, while Jesus is at the right hand of the Father. It's not that complex. He has never left us. He's always there for us. Just ask.

5

The Pursuit of Happiness

We have a God-given American right to pursue happiness. You might be thinking, "Well, that's a pretty bold statement." But it's not.

The preamble of the Declaration of Independence— which separated this nation from England in July 1776 and declared that we were going to be free—says that we have the inalienable right, given by our Creator, to life, liberty, and the pursuit of happiness. It is an American right to pursue happiness.

That's what most of us spend a lot of our time doing: pursuing happiness. We're looking for happiness all the time. The problem is, in life, we most often find ourselves feeling like what's described in Ecclesiastes 1:1-2:

The words of the Teacher, son of David, king of [Israel]: "Meaningless! Meaningless!" says the teacher. "Utterly meaningless! Everything is meaningless."

Instead of finding the pot of gold at the end of the rainbow, most of us come to a similar conclusion. We find out that everything we're doing, everything we're working for, and everything we do to pursue happiness is becoming meaningless.

I want you to read another version of this passage in Ecclesiastes because it will give you a couple of insights into the word "meaningless." So here's the New King James Version:

> *The words of the Preacher, the son of David, king of Jerusalem. "Vanity of vanities," says the preacher; "Vanity of vanities, all is vanity."*

When we take a look at the footnote for verse 2, we see that the word "vanity" means "empty." Another translation renders the phrase in verse 2, *"Absurdity, Absurdity. Everything is absurd."* One of my favorite renditions states this: *"Nonsense, nonsense. Everything is nonsense."*

But the absolute best rendition is this last one. I think you're going to agree with me on this: *"Frustration, oh, frustration. Oh, everything in life is just a tad bit frustrating."* Isn't this what life is actually like? We're taught that life is supposed to be happy, but sometimes it's just frustration after frustration.

And what do we usually do when things get frustrating? We decide that we're going to make ourselves happy. We're going to figure out the formula, and we're going to make ourselves happy because it's our right, guaranteed in the preamble to the Declaration of Independence.

So, in our pursuit of happiness, we start going to work, trying to figure it out. We decide that we're going to take a cooking class because that will make us happy. We're going to start a basketball league because that's what's going to make us happy. We're going to work out and become like Arnold Schwarzenegger because that will make us happy. We're going to join a bridge club and play cards because it will make us happy. As a husband and wife, we're going to have date night because date night will change everything.

And we'll always be happy. Does this sound familiar? These are the things that we do.

Has any of that ever worked for anybody? No! It has never worked for anybody ever, period. Every time we try to make ourselves happy, it's amazing how often we fail and feel farther away from happiness as a result. But somebody else went through this process and left us with the solution. His name was Solomon. He was the one who wrote the book of Ecclesiastes.

The great thing about Solomon is that he had the resources to do anything and everything he wanted to do. In the first chapter of Ecclesiastes, he reviews a few things he used to try to gain happiness, and then he lets us know the result of his pursuits.

Let's look at Ecclesiastes 1:12. This is what it says:

> *I, the teacher, was king over Israel in Jerusalem. I devoted myself to studying and exploring by wisdom all that is done under heaven. What a heavy burden God has laid on men! I have seen all the things that are done under the sun; all of them are meaningless, like chasing after the wind.*

The first thing Solomon decided to pursue was knowledge and wisdom. And if we pay attention to our world today, what we learn is—and this is going to ruffle a few feathers, but it's ok—education is everything. It's all about education. Why is that? Education is a great tool in and of itself. But education does not make you happy. You can be Dr. Fahrenheit with seven different degrees, and you still aren't going to be happy because that's not what makes people happy.

You can be wise beyond your years. You can be the Bible's answer, man, with a solution to everyone's problems. But it's not going to make you happy. Education is great. Children need to be educated. But you will not find happiness in your education. It won't happen.

Let's look at some of the other things Solomon decided to explore because there are many other good ones. This one from Ecclesiastes 2:1-3 is one every adult can relate to:

> *I thought in my heart, "Come now, I will test you with pleasure to find out what is good." But that also proved to be meaningless. "Laughter," I said, "is foolish. And what does pleasure accomplish?" So I tried cheering myself on with wine and embracing folly—my mind was still guiding me with wisdom. I wanted to see what was worthwhile for men to do under heaven during the few days of their lives.*

Guess what Solomon's talking about? Solomon's talking about partying. This was a king who had a great number of resources and vast quantities of wine. Napa Valley or Temecula Valley in California wine country can't even conceive of the amount of wine Solomon had access to. So Solomon drank from the start of the day to the end of the night. All he did was drink, drink, drink, drink, drink, drink, trying to find that happiness. But he never found it. It wasn't there in the party room. He couldn't find happiness in partying. Many of us have done this kind of thing (even if we as Christians don't talk about it much), but it's still not the answer to being happy.

What else did Solomon do to try and find happiness?

Let's look at verses 4-6:

> *I built houses for myself and planted vineyards. I made gardens and parks and planted all kinds of fruit trees in them. I made reservoirs to water groves of flourishing trees.*

Look what Solomon did. He lived the American dream. God bless him. He built houses. "All I want to do is build a house. All I want to do is own a house. That will make me happy." Does that sound familiar?

It won't make you happy. Solomon built some unbelievable houses. And yet, he wasn't happy. He built reservoirs. He built fruit orchards. He went far beyond any person had ever gone before. He had great personal accomplishments. Well, it didn't work. All he did was build monuments to himself. When he was building all these things, he thought,

"That will make me happy. Then people will remember me, and they'll know how great I am." But it didn't make him happy.

Let's look at verses 7-9. Here, Solomon is describing other pursuits of happiness:

> *I bought male and female slaves and had other slaves who were born in my house. I also owned more herds and flocks than anyone in Jerusalem before me. I amassed silver and gold for myself and the treasure of kings and provinces. I acquired men and women singers and a harem as well—the delights of the heart of man. I became greater by far than anyone in Jerusalem before me. In all this, my wisdom stayed with me.*

He says, "I had male and female slaves. I was in control." We think being in control makes us happy. But does it?

No, it doesn't make us happy. We want to be in control because we think if we've got everything in control and have all our ducks lined up, we'll be okay. But that will not make us happy.

Then he talks about amassing herds, gold, and silver. What does that represent? Money. Solomon thought, "Oh, but if I have money, I'll be happy." He had more money and wealth than anybody in history—past or present. In his day, silver was thought of as rocks. Try to imagine that. That's how wealthy Solomon and his kingdom were. But, of course, money did not make him happy.

What about the men and women singers Solomon described? What does that represent? Entertainment. Solomon wanted to be entertained, and so do we. We think, "Well, if I'm entertained, then I'll be happy. I've got a surround sound system and a big-screen TV." But that will not make me happy. It gives me moments of joy, but it will not make me happy.

Now, here's the big one Solomon struggled with. He says in verse 8

> *"I acquired men and women singers, and a harem as well—the delights of the heart of man."*

Let's just get this one straight. Sex will not make you happy. I know. You think it will. I know in your mind you're thinking, "Oh, yes. That will. Trust me." No, it won't. Solomon had 700 wives and 300 concubines. He had 1000 women to choose from. He could have had three women each day for a year. He thought that would satisfy his lust. But the bottom line is that sex did not make Solomon happy.

Solomon had it all. Nothing stood between him and his pursuit of happiness. So, what was his conclusion? Here it is in verses 10-11:

> *I denied myself nothing my eyes desired; I refused my heart no pleasure. But, on the contrary, my heart took delight in all my work, which was the reward for all my labor. Yet when I surveyed all that my hands had done and what I had toiled to achieve, everything was meaningless, like chasing after the wind; nothing was gained under the sun.*

Solomon sums up all those things that I just enumerated in verse 11. He says, "I've done everything that man can do, and life is a crock because none of it made me happy." He had it all, did it all and still found no happiness. Where can happiness be found, then?

God, in His mercy, gives Solomon the answers. We're going to look at two Scriptures, and we're going to answer the question. In the pursuit of happiness, where can happiness be found?

Look at Ecclesiastes 2:24:

> *A man can do nothing better than eat and drink and find satisfaction in his work. <u>This, too, I see, is from the hand of God</u>, for without him, who can eat or find enjoyment? To the*

> *man who pleases him, God gives wisdom, knowledge, and happiness.*

Now, let's read Ecclesiastes 3:12-13. Look at what he says:

> *I know that there is nothing better for men than being happy and doing good while they live. So that everyone may eat and drink and find satisfaction in all their toil—<u>this is the gift of God</u>.*

Do you see what Solomon concluded? You can do everything your heart desires. You can accomplish the greatest things. You can build great kingdoms. You can amass great fortunes. You can buy houses. You can have massive amounts of entertainment and sex. But none of that will make you happy. So what did Solomon learn through all his searching for happiness?

He learned that happiness is a gift from God. Period.

There is nothing that you can do to guarantee your happiness. You are not the creator. You are the creation. And you must yield to the Creator. And only through the Creator can creation find its perfect place.

You might be thinking, "But David, I'm trying so hard."

Good luck with that because it's never going to change. ***Only God can grant you the gift of happiness***. That's a hard lesson to accept. It's hard because I've been trying for so many years to do it on my own. And look what it's gotten me. Not happiness. And for all of you reading this, it's the same thing. You've been doing the same thing.

We all do the same thing because we will try anything that we can think of. We will give anything a shot—even a round of shots. And when we're not happy, we try to add this or that or do this or that. But it never works because happiness can only come as a gift from God, period.

There's no other way to find happiness. It is a gift. So how do we get this gift? Look at Ecclesiastes 12:13. God always gives us the answer. Here it is:

> *"Now all has been heard; here is the conclusion of the matter: Fear God and keep his commandments, for this is the whole duty of man."*

The word fear in Hebrew has multiple definitions. First, we hear that word, and we think it means something like "to tremble." But that's not what it means in this context. It means *to honor.*

That's one definition. Honor God. Honor him in your thoughts and your heart. Make sure that He receives honor from you and that you acknowledge Him.

Another definition is *respect*. Respect God. Don't disrespect God. Give him his just due. We respect the king. If a president walked into our church on Sunday, every person in attendance would stand in respect (almost every person, anyway). We need to do that and more out of respect for God.

The third definition is *to be in awe*. To fear God is to be in awe of God. It's to wake up in the morning, think about how great God is, and go, Wow. You are amazing. You're amazing, God."

The fourth definition of the word fear in Hebrew is *appreciation*. Appreciate God. God has done more for us than we will ever see or know. How many things has He done in your life that have protected you and you don't even know? He has saved your life a thousand times over. You don't even know it, but He's had your back many times.

So, you honor him. You respect him. You are in awe of him. And you appreciate him. <u>In this context, that's the fear of God.</u>

Verse 13 goes on to say, "and keep his commandments." We need to obey him. We make this so complex, so I'm going to simplify it right now. Obey God. Do what he wants you to do. That's not very complicated, is it?

What defines success in the Christian life? A Christian is not successful when they have a big ministry. A Christian is not successful when they have a big bank account. A Christian is not successful when they have a big family. A Christian is not successful when they have a big heart. **A Christian is successful when that Christian obeys God.** <u>God defines success by the word obedience</u>. It is better to obey than sacrifice. It is better to do what God wants you to do than put on a show. It's just easier. And God likes it that way.

With obedience in mind, let's do something that will put this in perspective because I want to obey God, and I want you to obey Him as well. I want us to do what He wants us to do. I don't always do what He wants me to do, <u>but I want to</u>.

The best way to obey God is to understand what the New Testament commandments are from God. So, let's close out the chapter by looking at Mark 12:28:

> *"One of the teachers of the law came and heard*
> *them debating. Noticing that Jesus had given*

> *them a good answer, he asked him, 'Of all the commandments, which is the most important?'"*

In the time of Christ, there were 619 (or 613, relax) commandments that the Pharisees had figured out; around 350-ish of them were negative commandments, and around 250-ish of them were positive. And they were always sitting around and debating what the most important commandments were from the list. So, this was not that uncommon of a question to ask somebody who was a teacher.

Here's how Jesus answered them in verses 29-31:

> *"The most important one," answered Jesus, "is this: 'Hear, O Israel, the Lord our God, the Lord is one. Love the Lord your God with all your heart, with all your soul, with all your mind and with all your strength.' The second is this: 'Love your neighbor as yourself.' There is no commandment greater than these."*

The summation of everything that God wants from us as Christians is in these three verses. The honor, respect, awe, and appreciation from Ecclesiastes are right here in the book of Mark. "Love the Lord your God with all your heart and with all your soul and with all your mind and with all your strength." What does your heart refer to? It refers to your feelings and emotions.

What is your soul? This is an interesting question. There's a lot of debate about this. The soul is essentially the center of who you are—your very inner being. What about loving God with all your mind? That means to love God with your thoughts, thinking thoughts towards God. And strength? That means with all your physical ability and with all your body. Your body is not your own. It's God's property.

Jesus says, "Love your neighbor as yourself." So, as you love yourself because you want yourself to be happy, that's how you should love your neighbor so that your neighbor is happy.

Then, a great question comes up. "Who is my neighbor?" In response, Jesus told that great parable about the Pharisee and the Sadducee who went by the man on the road who was wounded, but then the Samaritan who came along helped him instead of passing by.

After studying this parable for a long time, I've come up with a new answer for who my neighbor is. Some people argue that neighbors mean everyone everywhere. For example, there is somebody in Pakistan who lives on a street I've never seen. He's supposed to be my neighbor. But it's hard for me to be a neighbor to him because we're so far apart. So, who is my neighbor? ***Anyone that God brings into my life.* That's my neighbor.**

I need to love that person as I love myself, and I need to apply the Golden Rule: Do unto them as I would have them do unto me. Give to them as I would have somebody give to me. Love them the way that I want them to love me. I need to love them, and I need to love God.

And if I revere God—if I give Him honor and if I respect Him, if I'm in awe of Him and I appreciate Him, and I obey His commandments to love Him and to love my neighbor—**I've got a gift coming my way, and that gift is called <u>happiness</u>**. So it's time for Happy Land.

6

There is No Secret...

There's a movie out there called <u>The Secret</u>, and it's based on the Law of Attraction. The Law of Attraction is summed up like this: You see something in your mind. Then you speak it with your mouth, and you attract that thought to yourself. At first glance, it seems harmless, but there are big problems with it.

The origin of this philosophy comes from a book called <u>Ask, and It Is Given</u>. It sounds like a familiar Bible text, but in this case, one of the two people who wrote the book is a spiritualist who openly admits that she was channeling a spirit named Abraham. She claims that Abraham gave her the Laws of Attraction and the principles for gaining more wealth in life. This seemed like a great thing to so many people that even people with religious backgrounds jumped on board. The authors claimed to have found the secret of the universe.

The idea has an appeal or attraction to everyone because we have all gone through life looking for the secret sauce. Sometimes, it seems like money just runs away from us, and we're trying to figure out what we need to do to get it to come back to us. Then comes a book like this, and its promises tempt us. It's attractive. We think we need that. We think we might want to try self-actualization, self-empowerment, and all those sorts of ideas. They all sound like they can be very beneficial.

But every one of them, including <u>The Secret</u>, is wrong. Let's look at 1 Timothy 4:1. This will blow your mind.

> *The Spirit clearly says that some will abandon their faith in later times and follow deceiving spirits and things taught by demons.*

The Spirit (the Holy Spirit) clearly says that in later times, some will abandon their faith and follow deceiving spirits and things taught by demons. There is demonic doctrine. Some demons teach. They teach through other people. It sounds strange to us, doesn't it? It sounds strange until you realize that if there's a teaching that exalts man while at the same time removing God in any capacity, it's a demonic teaching.

You might be able to practice this unique "secret" philosophy, become rich beyond your dreams, and make your business work because you are accessing the secret of the universe. But if that's your situation, God is not at the center. Instead, you're following the doctrine of a demon.

Suppose you are following a doctrine that lies about the truth—that challenges biblical truth, which alters the image of God—and you buy into it. In that case, you are following the doctrine of a demon.

Look again at what verse 1 says. *The Spirit clearly says that in later times, some will abandon their faith and follow deceiving spirits and things taught by demons.* That's serious stuff. It's not a joke at all.

I had somebody at my workplace tell me I needed to watch *The Secret.* So, I spent about five minutes researching to find out about it. I learned that this was all about channeling a spirit. So, I went back to my coworker and said, "Dude, you are an idiot! Why would you watch that?"

And he asked me, "Is there a Christian version?" I said, "Yeah, but not like this."

The answer my coworker needed to hear is found in Philippians 4. I want you to know something: God is not stingy. He's not this sadistic being who's just trying to play your life out and make things miserable. That's just the bad image you've created in your mind. I want to tell you the truth. There is no "secret" to be found in these worldly philosophies and teachings.

Here is the truth, in Philippians 4:10-13:

> *I rejoiced greatly in the Lord that, at last, you renewed your concern for me. Indeed, you were concerned, but you had no opportunity to show it. I am not saying this because I am in need, for I have learned to be content whatever the circumstances. I know what it is to be in need, and I know what it is to have plenty. I have learned the secret of being content in any and every situation, whether well fed or hungry, whether living in plenty or in want. I can do all this through him, who gives me strength.*

Do you want to know the secret that's not really a secret? The secret isn't that you get to visualize, then call out, and then speak things into existence. When you do all these things on your own, you are in league with demons. You don't want to do that. So here's the secret: **In Jesus, you can do anything, <u>period</u>.**

You might say, "You don't know my situation." But the truth is, you don't know your God. He is a better Savior than you, sinner.

There's nothing wrong with being confident. As long as your confidence is found in Christ, there's nothing wrong with being successful. There's nothing wrong with being an overcomer as long as it's **with** God. There's nothing wrong with you using your abilities and skills to do things as long as everything **comes from Christ's power** and not yours.

There's nothing wrong with prosperity unless it excludes God, and God isn't given credit for the process. Do you understand that difference? It's not what we do with our philosophies, our little gimmicks, or our little formulas. It's us **with God**. That's the golden ticket.

You may think, "What about all those 'possibility' thinkers?" Jesus said all things are possible *to him who believes*. He didn't say all things are possible to him that believes in a system that's void of God. All things are possible to him who believes in God. The whole foundation is the believing in God part, and that's what people usually miss. That's where people make a mistake when they try to actualize stuff on their own. But you **can** accomplish anything through God. I'm going to show you that later in this chapter.

But first, I want to look at John 15. There's an opposite track to what I'm saying—another angle we need to see. Here's John 15:4:

> *Remain in me, as I also remain in you. No branch can bear fruit by itself; it must remain on the vine. Neither can you bear fruit unless you remain in me. "I am the vine; you are the branches. If you remain in me and I in you, you will bear much fruit; apart from me, you can do nothing.*

What do you mean, nothing?

I am a very confident and positive person in general. But that confidence is because of God. Because I trust in Him. But I am also smart enough to know that I know that there's a lot of yuck inside myself. In fact, every time I get closer to God, I start to realize how much more yuck there is in me. One of the most amazing things is when you start to realize how perfect Christ is. Everything he does has a good purpose and motive. And then you start doing that reflection of yourself. If we're honest about ourselves, we're nothing like that. The cleaner you become, the easier it is to see your own dirt. And in this passage, Jesus says, You can't do anything without me.

The gut check is that everything good comes through Christ. We can't do anything without him. We cannot succeed on an eternal basis. Without Christ, it is impossible. We can have temporary victories. But even sin is only pleasurable for a season, according to the Bible (Hebrews 11:25). But the season ends, and the result is death.

One time, I was running, and I was in deep prayer. My thoughts kept coming back to, "I can do anything for you, Lord." But the Spirit reminded me of the other verse, "You can do nothing without Me." I'm fine with the first verse. I can do anything through him. It feels great to realize that. But I also need to acknowledge that I can do nothing without Him. It's humbling to live out that truth.

These false doctrines found in books like <u>Ask and It Is Given</u> and movies like <u>The Secret</u> focus on **the self**. It's about you gaining wealth or something else. It's always about gaining something in your own power. Here's the great thing, though: **In God, you can find contentment**, and God doesn't mind you being wealthy as long as your wealth is used for a purpose and doesn't become an idol. What I'm trying to convey is that everything is through Jesus, and nothing is without Him. How do we know that's true?

Look at James 4. This is for those of us who engage in business, dreams, and wisdom and love all our insights and brilliance. Here's James 4:13-17:

> *Now listen, you who say, "Today or tomorrow we will go to this or that city, spend a year there, carry on business and make money." Why do you not even know what will happen tomorrow? What is your life like? You are a mist that appears for a little while and then vanishes. Instead, you ought to say, "If it is the Lord's will, we will live and do this or that." As it is, you boast about your arrogant schemes. All such boasting is evil. If anyone, then, knows the good they ought to do and doesn't do it, it is a sin for them.*

Here's what the passage is saying—everything through Jesus, nothing without Jesus. We can make a plan that we're going to go somewhere for a year, or we're going to do this or that. We're going to create a business. We're going to reach a certain goal. All of that is great unless God decides to drop an atomic bomb on your head tomorrow, and then all those plans are gone. So, there must be submission to the power and the will of God.

There's nothing wrong with hoping. There's nothing wrong with dreaming. There's nothing wrong with believing unless you're doing it **apart**

from God. In that case, we're just exalting man and denying God. That's exactly what happened in the Garden of Eden. We always tell ourselves, "If I were in the garden, I wouldn't do it." But we commit the exact same sin all the time. Do you know what sin is? The snake said, "*If you eat that, you'll be like God.*" That is a terrible deception, but we're still falling for it today.

I must remember that everything is through Jesus; nothing is without him.

Check out Acts 17:24-28:

> *The God who made the world and everything in it is the Lord of heaven and earth and does not live in temples built by human hands. And he is not served by human hands, as if he needed anything. Rather, he gives everyone life, breath, and everything else. From one man, he made all the nations so that they should inhabit the whole earth, and he marked out their appointed times in history and the boundaries of their lands. God did this so that they would seek him and perhaps reach out for him and find him, though he is not far from any one of us. 'For in him we live and move and have our being.' As some of your own poets have said, 'We are his offspring.'*

There is not a thing—a man, a woman, a child, a dog, a cat, a bird, or a fish—that has ever accomplished anything apart from God. Now, there are many things that people and animals have accomplished, even cool things. However, they take the sole credit. But it is God who determines **everyone, and everything's very breath**.

So, that breath you just took—who gave it to you? God. If God didn't want to give you a breath, you wouldn't be breathing, and you would die. So, there's nothing you have ever accomplished in life that you did independent of God, **period**.

All these systems of man and spirits are trying to create greatness in us when the only greatness that's really there is the one that comes through God. You get that greatness by acknowledging that you can't do anything without God.

And what you need to do to acknowledge that truth is to put God at the center of everything.

The question, though, is: why? Why does God say everything through Him and nothing without Him? What is he doing? Why is that the setup?

This is the key to the whole message. And it's no secret. God wants you to do everything through Him and nothing without Him because God wants to be our partner in everything.

He doesn't want you to have a single area in life that He and you are not partnering in.

Look at 1 Corinthians 3:9. I want you to see this one small word that means so much:

> *"For we are coworkers in God's service; you are God's field, God's building."*

You are God's coworker; you're His partner. He wants to partner with you in everything. Now, I want you to read Mark 16:19-20. This is a beautiful example of the heart of God in relation to us:

> *After the Lord Jesus had spoken to them, he was taken up into heaven, and he sat at the right hand of God. Then the disciples went out and preached everywhere, and the Lord worked with them and confirmed his word by the signs that accompanied it.*

God was working with the apostles. It was a partnership. It's all supposed to be a partnership. All of it. That's why He doesn't want you to go seeking self-empowerment. He wants you to seek everything through Him and nothing without Him.

I want to say something that I've never said before. **I want to describe the answer to everything in life.** Let's read Exodus 33:12-21:

Moses said to the Lord, "You have been telling me, 'Lead these people,' but you have not let me know whom you will send with me. You have said, 'I know you by name, and you have found favor with me.' If you are pleased with me, teach me your ways, so I may know you and continue to find favor with you. Remember that this nation is your people.

The Lord replied, My presence will go with you, and I will give you rest.

Then Moses said to him, If your presence does not go with us, do not send us up from here. How will anyone know that you are pleased with your people and with me unless you go with us? What else will distinguish your people and me from all the other people on the face of the earth?

And the Lord said to Moses, I will do the very thing you have asked because I am pleased with you, and I know you by name. Then Moses said, Now show me your glory.

And the Lord said, I will cause all my goodness to pass in front of you, and I will proclaim my name, the Lord, in your presence. I will have mercy on whom I will have mercy, and I will have compassion on whom I will have *compassion. But," he said, "you cannot see my face, for no one may see me and live.*

Then the Lord said, There is a place near me where you may stand on a rock. Then, when my glory passes by, I will put you in a cleft in the rock and cover you with my hand until I have passed by. Then I will remove my hand, and you will see my back, but my face must not be seen.

Moses is talking directly with God, face-to-face. He has been given instructions from God. He leads at least six hundred thousand people (some estimates are one million, eight hundred thousand people, give or take) from one place to another. He has been empowered. He has miracles at his disposal. This is a very, very powerful individual. He is so close to God. What does he say at that moment?

Show me your glory.

This is the answer to every issue alive in humanity, period.

Because Moses, who is exceedingly close to God, had a request. The request was in four letters: **MORE**. He wanted more of God. He wanted to see more. He wanted to know more. He wanted to understand more.

This is the solution to life. It's the bottom line. The solution is to have more of God in our lives so that we can walk with the living hope that comes from God. But, you see, the living hope that comes from God is eternal and situational.

So, in every single circumstance, the closer you get to God, the more you can walk in His gift of living hope in everything.

I don't know what your situation is. It doesn't even matter. But I know that the living hope from God is the answer, which He wants to pour out in you through a partnership with Him. He'll be glad to give it to you because you can't do anything apart from Him, and you can do everything through Him.

The reason that you'll prevail is that He's your partner. You can do anything through him. You don't need to use some fake human system to create this or that in your life. You don't need to use demonic divination and other things to make your life work. You have everything you possibly need in Christ. **You just need more of Him in everything.**

7

The Jehoshaphat Jam

Israel was made up of 12 tribes. After King Solomon, Rehoboam, who was Solomon's son, was put in place over Israel. The people came to Rehoboam and said, "You know, your dad was pretty cool with us, and we want to see if you're going to be cool, too. We want to see what's going to happen."

So Rehoboam got together with counselors who were his age. He also got together with counselors from the time of his father, Solomon. And they gave different counsel. Being as immature as he was, Rehoboam went with the counsel of the people of his own age instead of the counsel of the older people. So, he came back to the 12 tribes of Israel, and he said, "When you served my father, he was a really good king, but he wasn't very tough. I am going to be so tough that it's going to seem like my pinky is like my father's thigh. That's how tough I'm going to be." Well, 10 of the 12 tribes said,

"Forget it. We're out of here." So they rebelled, and they took off, and they split Israel as a nation. So, the ten tribes that split off on this side became known as the Northern tribes, and the two that stayed together—Judah and Benjamin—became known as the Southern tribes. So, it was what we call a divided kingdom. And there were two separate entities (even though the overall concept is that they were Israel), were split up.

The Northern tribe never had any good kings. One king after another was just as bad as the next one. It was awful. But the Southern tribe, which was David's and Solomon's tribe, had a situation where one king was a real yutz, and then one king was really good. So, they alternated kings like that throughout their history.

I want to talk about a time when Jehoshaphat was king of the Southern tribes. He was one of the good guys. Let's read 2 Chronicles 20:1-2:

> *After this, the people of Moab, with the people of Ammon, and others with them besides the Ammonites, came to battle against Jehoshaphat. Then some came and told Jehoshaphat, saying, "A great multitude is coming against you from beyond the sea, from Syria; and they are in Hazazon Tamar" (which is En Gedi).*

I want you to catch what is happening. Jehoshaphat's doing pretty well as a king. He's trying to follow the Lord. Then somebody comes along and says, "Guess what, Jehoshaphat? There is an enormous army that is coming against your land. Three different countries have gotten together, and they are coming to take away all your spoils and take your land. What are you going to do?"

We have situations in our personal lives where armies come up against us. It may be that you are in a situation where you feel that you are being surrounded and overwhelmed, and you don't know how to handle it. You may be going through emotions that are ripping you apart inside so much that you're not sure how to approach them. It's like an army coming against you.

You may be struggling with a personal sin that you can't seem to beat. And it comes up against you every time you take a step forward, and it tries to beat you down and rob you. So whatever the armies are, they are coming up against us and pressing in, and we need to know what to do. We need to know how to respond.

Jehoshaphat had this very situation in a very literal sense. I want you to know how big this opposing army was. Scholars have estimated that there could have been anywhere from 750,000 to 1,000,000 people coming against Jehoshaphat. That's a lot. And he didn't do anything wrong. He's just being old, Jehoshaphat. His people think he's a nice king. Everybody thinks he's great. But the devil never sits still. He is a defeated foe, but he is not sleeping on his bed. He is at work.

Let's look at verses 3-4:

> *And Jehoshaphat feared, set himself to seek the LORD, and proclaimed a fast throughout all of Judah. So Judah gathered together to ask for help from the LORD, and from all the cities of Judah, they came to seek the LORD.*

Now, many of us—who have armies that are coming against us in whatever capacity—try to figure out every single angle within us to stop those armies from coming against us. We run through every ounce of energy and wisdom we have. **Then, after we have depleted everything within our very being**, we go into the closet. We closed it. We get down on our hands and knees, and we plead, "Oh, help me, God. Please help me, God."

Jehoshaphat had a lot more sense than we modern folk usually do because he did not wait until he depleted all that he was and had. Instead, he did something so novel and unusual: *He sought*

<u>*God first*</u>. Jehoshaphat was going through a struggle, and he sought the face of God first, not last.

Whether you are in the middle of a Jehoshaphat army situation, or whether you are about to enter one, or whether you have just come out of one, no matter where you're at, **why don't you and I go into the closet and seek the face of God first, not last?** Then, we will get the insight that we need to fight the battle.

Now, here's what Jehoshaphat did. In verses 5-12, we see what we call the prayer of dependence. Let's read this:

> *Jehoshaphat stood in the assembly of Judah and Jerusalem, in the house of the LORD, before the new court, and said, "O LORD God of our fathers, are You not God in heaven, and do You not rule over all the kingdoms of the nations, and in Your hand is there not power and might, so that no one can withstand You? Are You not our God, who drove out the inhabitants of this land before Your people Israel and gave it to the descendants of Abraham, Your friend forever? And they dwell in it and have built You a sanctuary in it for Your name, saying, 'If disaster comes upon us—–sword, judgment, pestilence, or famine––we*

> *will stand before this temple and in Your presence (for Your name is in this temple), and cry out to You in our affliction, and You will hear and save.' "And now, here are the people of Ammon, Moab, and Mount Seir–– whom You would not let Israel invade when they came out of the land of Egypt, but they turned from them and did not destroy them––here they are, rewarding us by coming to throw us out of Your possession, which You have given us to inherit. O our God, will You not judge them? For we have no power against this great multitude that is coming against us, nor do we know what to do, but our eyes are upon You."*

There are two huge lessons I want you to take away from these verses. Jehoshaphat's **first step** in seeking the Lord is to acknowledge that God is in charge above and beyond everything else. I want to give you the best advice you could ever start with ...when you're in a similar situation. You need to start off by acknowledging that God is ultimately in control.

The demons are not in control. Satan is not in control. We are not in control. The circumstances are not in our control. People who shout loudly are not in control. **God is in control**. That's where we should start. No matter how brilliant we think our evaluation of the circumstances is, and how it came to be, we need to start off by humbly acknowledging that God Almighty is on the throne at the center of the universe.

Everything revolves around Him because He is the core of all things.

Here's **the second** really important lesson from this story. It helps us know what our disposition should be when the armies are coming up against us. Verse 12 says this:

> *"O our God, will You not judge them? For we have no power against this great multitude that is coming against us."*

The Bible says that God opposes the proud but gives grace to the humble. The word "opposes" means "fights against." God fights against people who are full of pride and arrogance. God is not going to fight for us in a situation where we are arrogant and prideful.

He fights against the proud. So, when we acknowledge that He is in charge, **the next thing we need to do is acknowledge that we aren't.** We need to make sure that the Lord is in charge and that we give up the lordship of our own lives in favor of the wisdom, compassion, mercy, and direction of God.

If we can do these things, we are going to be triumphant.

(1) We see Jehoshaphat seeking the face of God first. Then, (2) we see him acknowledging God as the one in charge. Next (3), we see him acknowledge that he has no strength on his own. Then he makes this statement: (4) "Nor do we know what to do." Jehoshaphat has no idea what to do.

Do you know how many times in counseling I have heard, "I don't know what to do?" Do you know how many times a day I say that to myself? I don't know what to do. If the light is green, I know what to do. But I'm talking about when things are tough. I'm talking about when my own sin beats me up, and I can't seem to overcome it. I don't know what to do.

But Jehoshaphat makes it clear when he says, "***but our*** eyes are upon You."

Here is the answer: *Our eyes are upon the Lord.* The answer is a fixed vision of God. When you don't know what to do, fix your vision on God. Don't look anywhere else. Don't look to the left. Don't look to the right. Don't look in the mirror. Don't look to the government. Fix your vision on God.

Hebrews chapter 12:2 says this: "*Looking unto Jesus, the author and finisher of our faith.*" Our gaze is to be fixed on God.

> *Isaiah chapter 26:3 says this: "You will keep him in perfect peace, whose mind is stayed on You because he trusts in You."*

You go through these situations, and you don't know what to do. And I understand that completely because neither do I. But the answer is: **We fix our vision on God**. We don't let the circumstances become the vision. We don't let the feelings become the vision. We don't let sin become the vision. We don't let the failure become the vision. We don't let Satan become the vision. We don't let people become the vision.

So God is where we fix our eyes—got that?

Now, God has something to say. Recall the sequence here. The armies are against Jehoshaphat. He seeks God first (**1**). Then he acknowledges that God is in charge (**2**). Third, he acknowledges that he has no strength of his own (**3**). Finally, he acknowledges he doesn't know what to do, but he fixes his vision on God (**4**).

Here's God's response in 2 Chronicles 20:15:

> *And he said, "Listen, all you of Judah and you inhabitants of Jerusalem, and you, King Jehoshaphat! Thus says the Lord to you: 'Do not be afraid nor dismayed because of this great multitude, for the battle is not yours, but God's.'*

The first thing that God says after Jehoshaphat's done all these great things, and he's walking so right and so perfectly, is, "**Do not be afraid**." Do not fear these armies. Do not fear these feelings. Do not fear the sin. Do not fear Satan. Do not fear people. Do not fear difficult situations. Do not fear what is coming against you. Do not be afraid.

<u>We need to remember this as Christians.</u>

Zechariah 2:8 says that you are the apple of God's eye. He does not look upon you with displeasure. He does not look upon you with disdain. He does not look upon you with discouragement. He does not look at you and frown. Instead, He looks upon you with absolute pleasure and delight. He loves you. He delights in you. You are the flower in his heart. You are the whole shebang to God. Everything He is doing on this earth is for your benefit. **You are his passion**.

Yes, He's still working on the sin and getting the bad stuff out of your life, but you have eternity with Him to look forward to. He's taking all of us into eternity because He loves us and wants to be around us. He's putting all our homes together so that we can be around him. He's moving all His family into His country, so to speak because He loves us. Cool.

This same God is not angry at you every time you think, "Oh, I've done this wrong. Now God doesn't like me." That is just a ploy of the enemy to draw you away from the Father, who is passionately in love with you every moment. He's fighting **for you**, not <u>against you</u>.

Sometimes, he fights, and you don't even know He's fighting for you. He goes before you in a way you cannot yet imagine. I would bet everything I have that God has gone before you and prevented disasters in ways you cannot grasp or comprehend. Why? We are finite, and He is infinite. And you can't fit infinite into a finite box. A square peg doesn't go into a round hole. Okay, you get what I am saying.

God's passion for us is here: "**Don't be afraid. I'm fighting for you. I'm taking care of business.**"

So now we come to the key object lesson from this passage. We all need to understand this and put it into practice in our lives. Look at 2 Chronicles 20:18-21:

Jehoshaphat bowed his head with his face to the ground, and all Judah and the inhabitants of Jerusalem bowed before the LORD, worshiping the LORD. Then the Levites of the children of the Kohathites and of the children of the Korahites stood up to praise the LORD God of Israel with voices loud and high.

So they rose early in the morning and went out into the wilderness of Tekoa. As they went out, Jehoshaphat stood and said, "Hear me, O Judah and you inhabitants of Jerusalem: Believe in the LORD your God, and you shall be established; believe His prophets, and you shall prosper."

And when he had consulted with the people, he appointed those who should sing to the LORD and who should praise the beauty of holiness, as they went out before the army and were saying, 'Praise the LORD, for His mercy endures forever.

Jehoshaphat teaches us that we need to face the armies in our lives <u>with praise on our lips</u>! We go into battle praising. We don't go in wondering. We don't go in doubting. We don't go in fear. We go in with a spirit of praise because of the commitment that God has given us. Because of the passion God has for you, you have acknowledged Him as in charge.

We throw ourselves at His feet, and we fix our vision on Him alone. God says to us, "Do not be afraid," and then we go into battle worshipping and praising the Lord, acknowledging Him as the king.

That's how we do it.

Saul, after he became king, had a few problems with rebellion and sin. God had to do something about that. At some point, Saul inherited an evil spirit, and the spirit would make Saul do goofy things. So the leaders said, "What are we going to do? The king's got an evil spirit. He's still got to run the nation."

The leaders decided, "We've got to get him a musician. Let him sing songs." So they got a musician to come and play music and sing songs for King Saul. Guess who they picked? David.

And so David went into Saul's palace, and he started playing his harp and singing songs. What happened to the spirit that was harassing Saul? See you later, alligator, because demonic spirits hate worship. Satan is constantly trying to steal worship from God. So when David came in and started worshipping the Lord, Satan was thinking, "This is exactly the opposite of what we want to be around. We'll see you later." And the evil spirits left Saul.

How do we know that David played worship songs?

Read the Psalms, the Songs of David.

Do you know how much power there is in praise? I'm not talking about fantasy power. When you release your faith and acknowledge God, you had better step back. Big things are going to happen.

Isaiah 61:3 says this: ***"[Put on a] garment of praise for the spirit of heaviness."*** Are you ever overwhelmed? Do you want to watch your whole countenance change? Do you want to watch your whole internal being shift?

Put on the garment of praise and watch the spirit of heaviness be destroyed. When we get into heaven, we're going to go in praising Him. And when the Lord comes, with the angels, they are going to come out praising. How powerful is that?

Jehoshaphat nailed it right away. He confronted his army situation with praise on his lips. There is power in praise that you can access at any time.

Do you want to see victory in spiritual warfare? Fill the air with praise. The entire purpose of Satan is an attempt to take away the praise that only God deserves. Even Satan said, "I will be like the most high." *I will be like...* He wanted to be exalted to the level of God so that he could receive the praise. When he couldn't win with the angels, he then tried to sucker in Adam and Eve with the same thing. He offered for them to "be like God."

And if Satan's goal is to steal praise, then the very thing that breaks Satan is pure, sincere worship of the Lord. And do you know why man was created? **To fellowship, worship, glorify, and enjoy God forever**. So, do you want to rip apart the kingdom of Satan? Learn to be a worshipper and say, "Thanks to God," under every circumstance (1 Thessalonians 5:18). You'll blow Satan's kingdom down, and he will flee (James 4:7).

Turning back now to 2 Chronicles 20, look what happened in Jehoshaphat's situation when the people began to praise in verses 22-23:

> *When they began to sing and praise, the Lord set ambushes against the people of Ammon, Moab, and Mount Seir, who had come against Judah, and they were defeated. The people of Ammon and Moab stood up against the inhabitants of Mount Seir to utterly kill and destroy them. And when they had made an end to the inhabitants of Seir, they helped to destroy one another. So when Judah came to a place overlooking the wilderness, they looked toward the multitude, and there were their dead bodies, fallen on the earth. No one had escaped.*

In his army situation, Jehoshaphat came in praising. And do you know what happened when they first looked down into the wilderness area? There were thousands upon thousands of dead bodies scattered on the ground. So when you yield to God's control and praise Him, you'll have total victory. I'm not talking about partial—but total victory.

> *Romans 8:37 says, "In all these things we are more than conquerors through Him who loved us."*

> *2 Corinthians 2:14 says, "Now thanks be unto God, who always causes us to triumph."*

When we yield to God's control and praise Him with our lips, victory will come our way. God will go before us and wipe out, eradicate, and take care of whatever enemies we are facing so that when we get to that place, we can just look up and say, **"Thanks."** <u>There won't be anything else to say</u>.

I might not know how hard your particular circumstance is. I only know how hard my circumstances are. But I know that God is greater than any circumstance or situation. So when we face those armies in our lives, let's do what Jehoshaphat did. Let's seek God's help first, with praise on our lips, and watch the hand of the Lord bring victory into our lives.

Pathways to His Presence

Nehemiah 8:8-10 says this:

They read from the Book of the Law of God, making it clear and giving meaning so that the people understood what was being read.

Then Nehemiah the governor, Ezra the priest and teacher of the law, and the Levites who were instructing the people said to them all, "This day is holy to the Lord your God. Do not mourn or weep." All the people had been weeping as they listened to the words of the law.

Nehemiah said, "Go and enjoy choice food and sweet drinks, and send some to those who have nothing prepared. This day is holy to our Lord. Do not grieve, for the joy of the Lord is your strength."

The Levites, Ezra and Nehemiah, were instructing the people in the Word of God. Unfortunately, when the Bible is read aloud in too many churches, it's often used to bash people in the head with the Scriptures to make them feel bad. The pastor will say, "Well, you're not doing this, and you're not doing that, you sinner! And you're a bad example. So nanny, nanny, boo, boo." Right about that maturity level.

Here's the irony from one of the greatest texts **about** the Word of God and the purpose of the instruction: Nehemiah says to the people, "Don't grieve. Don't be upset. Don't cry." And in the people's minds, they're thinking, "But we're hearing what the Lord wants us to do, and we're not living up to everything we're supposed to do." So Nehemiah agrees *but* tells them, "You're hearing what the Lord wants—what He wants you to work on. He's not telling you this to beat you down. **He's telling you this to help you get closer to Him**."

The Word of God and the instructions in the Word of God are not given to you to destroy your spirit. It's not there to heap guilt on you. The Bible is not supposed to be used as ammunition to shoot people.

The purpose of the Word of God is to help us draw closer in our relationship with God.

1. The Bible illuminates a better understanding of God the Father.

2. The Bible helps us reflect Jesus Christ more and more. The Bible teaches us to walk in the fullness of the Holy Spirit.

God does not just perpetually deem you guilty. That doesn't take much to do. He's trying to teach you. He's trying to instruct you like a good parent teaches a child when they're doing something wrong.

Then Nehemiah makes this statement: "*The joy of the Lord is our strength.*" It is a tremendous principle from God. It's not just some cheesy song you sing in church as kids. But the people listening to Nehemiah didn't understand the principle at all. They didn't know what to do with those words. We still have the same problem today. If the joy of the Lord is our strength, what else do we need to know?

Psalm 16:11 says this:

You make known to me the path of life.

You will fill me with joy in your presence, with eternal pleasures at your right hand.

In Nehemiah, we hear that *the joy of the Lord is our strength.* In the Psalms, it says *your presence brings about the fullness of joy.* So, I'm going to give you a little math formula. This is the key to you and me walking in strength: if the joy of the Lord is our strength and the presence of the Lord is where that joy comes from, then we need the presence of the Lord to have the joy of the Lord. **That's where the power is.**

If you turn the television on for 15 minutes, you know we need strength. No matter what channel you turn to, you see the terrible situations we're in as a country. We need strength to make it. In order to gain strength, we need the joy of the Lord. In order to get the joy of the Lord, we need to be in his presence.

How do we find our pathways to the presence of God? How do we get the fullness of His presence? We can get there through personal examination and exploration of **various Biblical principles**. But what works for me may not work for you at the same engagement level. So, I want to quickly highlight seven Biblical ways that people can access the presence of God. Some of these may apply to you, or you may have something a little bit different.

First off, let's take a look at Psalm 22:3. It says:

But You art holy, O You that <u>inhabits</u> the praises of Israel.

The presence of God inhabits, dwells, or lives in the praises of His people. So, when you are a praising person, God's hanging out where those praises are, and you're hanging out in the presence of the Lord. What are they doing in heaven right now? They're not sitting on clouds. They're not reading the same magazine over and over again. They're praising God, and God is right there in the middle of it. So when you worship, you connect to heaven, where the presence of God dwells. That's a tremendous blessing.

Sometimes, you see people having a very emotional experience when they worship. But if you asked them what the pathway to the presence of the Lord is, I'm 99% certain they'll say worship. Well, why is that? Because that close connection to the presence gives them joy, and that joy gives them strength.

Other people get a tremendous amount of experience and engagement with God in His Word.

2 Timothy 3:16 says this:

All Scripture is God-breathed and is useful for teaching, rebuking, correcting, and training in righteousness.

The principle for God-breathed is the same concept as when God breathed into Adam—who was a lifeless piece of clay—and Adam became a living, breathing being. The same breath that was used to create Adam was also used to create the Scriptures. When you read the Bible, the breath of God falls upon you, and it's just like the breath of God falling upon Adam (Job 33:4). New life emerges because you're having an interaction with God's very breath.

The third pathway to God's presence is found in the book of Revelation.

Let's look at Revelation 5:6-8:

Then I saw a Lamb, looking as if it had been slain, standing at the center of the throne, encircled by the four living creatures and the elders. The Lamb had seven horns and seven eyes, which are the seven spirits of God sent out into all the earth. He went and took the scroll from the right hand of him, who sat on the throne. And when he had taken it, the four living creatures and the twenty-four elders fell down before the lamb. Each one had a harp, and they were holding golden bowls full of incense, which are the prayers of God's people.

Prayers, which are brought right into the very throne room of God, connect you to heaven by ripping and tearing the very fabric of the earth and allowing glimpses of heaven to break through.

Sometimes, you're praying, and you really get the sense that *this is serious.* That's the tearing apart of the fabric of the earth and the heavens reaching out and letting us know that there's a connection right then. That is the manifested presence of God (not the universal presence of God). And we're thinking, "Wow, that's awesome!" Does it happen all the time? No, <u>not for me</u>, but it does happen.

Sometimes, it's that one prayer where you go off by yourself and start crying, and nobody knows. It's just you and God. That's a tear in the fabric of the earth, with heaven reaching between the two. That's a pathway to the presence of God.

One of the most famous pathways to God's presence is found in Matthew 18:20:

Where two or three gather in my name, I am with them.

Jesus said this so we would know that God's presence is current when we fellowship. When you hug and pray for one another and listen together, there's a sense of togetherness and unity that develops. Some people can't live without fellowship. They want to hang out and love everybody. That's awesome. Too bad we are not all like that. God loves our fellowship, which is done in His name.

Another pathway to presence is service. In Matthew 28:19-20, Jesus said this:

> *Go and make disciples of all nations, baptizing them in the name of the Father, of the Son, and of the Holy Spirit, and teaching them to obey everything I have commanded you. And surely I am with you always, to the very end of the age."*

God is with people who serve Him. Serving as a Christian is a perfect pathway to the presence of God because, when you serve, you're reflecting Jesus, the Servant. God's reward for that is **His presence.**

Creation is another way we can experience God's presence. Notice I didn't use the word nature.

In Exodus 24:12, God said this to Moses:

Come up to me on the mountain and stay here, and I will give you the tablets of stone with the law and commandments I have written for their instruction.

God's presence includes interacting with His creation. For example, Jesus went out into the wilderness. He was hanging out with God in the wilderness. Just like Jesus, we can experience God's presence in His creation.

This next pathway is one of my favorites. But, first, look at what Paul says about Jesus in Ephesians 2:17-18:

He came and preached peace to those of you who were far away and peace to those who were near. For through him, we both have access to the Father through one Spirit.

I recognize that one of the ways that people have failed to access the pathway to God is that they aren't cultivating a relationship with the Holy Spirit (2 Corinthians 13:14). The Holy Spirit is the part of God that communes and lives inside you and empowers you and everything else in the Kingdom. People have such a hard time with this, though. The Holy Spirit is also called 'the One who guides us.'

He will guide us into all truth. The Holy Spirit is also called 'the Counselor.' So, watch this. The Holy Spirit is your guidance counselor. You should have a relationship with the Holy Spirit. Why? Because that access to the presence of God enables you to experience the joy of the Lord, which gives you strength.

Those are seven pathways to God's presence. If you're doing all seven perfectly, that's great. I tend to move quickly from pathway to pathway.

Have you ever noticed that if you're a person who's involved in any of those pathways, they're here today and gone tomorrow? Have you ever noticed that you're doing great, your spirit feels great, and you're so happy? Then you walk out the door, and you think, "Oh, shoot." And then it's just gone. It's all disappeared.

King David said to the Lord, "*Restore unto me the joy of my salvation.*" Have you ever experienced that joy? You've had that presence; you've had that awesome connection to God, and then five seconds later, somebody cuts you off on the freeway, and then it's all gone? That's when many of us lose the joy of the Lord. It becomes the OY of the Lord.

To be honest, we don't lose joy. But the truth is, there's a thief who is constantly trying to steal our joy.

When your joy gets stolen, here's what you need to do: <u>Go back to where you got it the first time</u>.

We need to go back into the presence of God a thousand times, if necessary, to get it back and walk in it. So go worship (**1**), read your Bible (**2**), pray (**3**), fellowship (**4**), serve (**5**), walk with the Lord in creation (**6**), or spend time with the Holy Spirit (**7**) and see if you can recapture what was stolen from you.

The key is that you must keep going back.

Our joy is going to be challenged continuously and sought to be stolen. So, we need to continuously go back and keep accessing God's presence. When we do that, we'll always be able to experience the joy of the Lord, and our strength will be renewed.

9

From Bad to Rad

Abraham was a man God called out of the country he was living in. He was also called out of the lifestyle he was living. Thus calling him to another land that God had promised him but that he had not yet seen. In the process, God had made him a promise. And from the promise was born a young man named Isaac.

Isaac represented, **literally**, the promises of God. So, every time I think of that name, I think of the promises of God.

Isaac had two sons, Esau, and Jacob. Out of Jacob came 12 sons. One of them was named Joseph. And that's who I want to talk about in this message.

Joseph was a favored child in the eyes of God. Now, the other 11 brothers didn't exactly perceive Joseph as a favored child. As a matter of fact, what would happen is that the other brothers would be working, and Joseph would watch what they were doing and then go back <u>and tell them</u>. "They are not doing this or that." That kind of thing. So, it did not ingratiate him with his brothers very much, and they didn't think very highly of him.

On top of that, their dad Jacob had this wonderful jacket designed with amazing colors that he gave to Joseph. Joseph was the favored kid. God was giving him dreams. He was giving him prophetic dreams. Joseph was doing well. Things were going great.

One day, he went out to see his brothers, wearing his fancy coat. He shared about the dreams he was having, and they lost them. They couldn't handle it. So they decided that they were going to kill him. So, they grabbed him, and they were getting ready to kill him. Reuben breaks with the wolf pack and says, "No, no, no. You can't kill him. Let's throw him into the water tank." Something along those lines because he didn't want to have his brother killed. So instead of killing Joseph, they sold him (Never forget; buy wholesale, sell retail).

Then, after being sold by his brothers, he eventually gets sold a second time to Potiphar, the captain of Pharaoh's court. Joseph becomes a diligent servant. He's a really good guy. But Potiphar's wife starts making the moves. Joseph tried to sidestep the situation. Joseph is telling her, "You know, your husband has brought me into his house. He's put me in charge of his household, and you're trying to get me to have intimate relations with you, and this would be bad, and this is wrong."

But Potiphar's wife kept trying to hit on him, and Joseph kept on trying to sidestep the situation and get out of the picture. Well, one time, she caught him alone in the house, and the situation was so bad that he had to run away. ***The only thing he could do was run because he didn't know what else to do.*** On his way out, she grabs his cloak, and off he goes. Now Joseph is naked, but he hasn't done anything wrong, has he? He is running away from trouble. He's trying to stay away from a problem. He's avoiding it.

Have fun with that, Joe.

After he runs away, Potiphar's wife goes to her husband and says, "Hey, hey, hey. You brought the Jewish kid in here. He's making the moves on me. Look at this. Can you believe it?"

Potiphar is livid. "Oh, I can't believe it." He's so mad.

So, he grabs Joseph and throws him in jail.

Here's Joseph's life up to this point: He gets sold. He gets falsely accused. He gets thrown in jail, and all because

a) God gave him a couple of dreams;

b) his dad gave him a coat; and

c) he was a little spoiled. This is not working out well for Joseph.

Now, he is in jail, and the jailer does him a favor. He is interpreting dreams, and eventually, Pharaoh has a dream. However, Pharaoh's dream troubles him, and the person serving Pharaoh his wine says, "Oh, I know this dude that interprets dreams. He's in jail. You should hear him. He'll interpret this for you."

Pharaoh then shares the dream with Joseph, and Joseph tells him the dream.

Joseph is probably standing there thinking, "Let's see. I tried to run away from Potiphar's wife. I got in trouble there. My brothers sold me. So now I'm going to tell Pharaoh a dream. Then he's going to take my head off and use it for a soccer ball."

But that's not what happened, is it? Let's take a look at some verses from Genesis 50. At this point in the story, Joseph's father has died, and his brothers need help. Still, they figure that their brother, who they sold and who is now managing Egypt's day-to-day affairs, is going to punish them for what they did.

Verse 15: "When Joseph's brothers saw that their father was dead, they said, 'What if Joseph holds a grudge against us and pays us back for all the wrongs we did to him?'"

The only real wrong recorded in the Bible is that they sold him and lied about it. That's bad, but there may have been other things that the brothers did that were not cool with Joseph. They were scared to see him.

Verse 16: "So they sent word to Joseph, saying, 'Your father left these instructions before he died:'"

Now, <u>we don't know if this is true or not</u>. But here is what they tell Joseph:

"'This is what you are to say to Joseph: I ask you to forgive your brothers the sins and the wrongs they committed to treating you so badly.' Now please forgive the sins of the servants of the God of your father." When their message came to him, Joseph wept. His brothers then came and threw themselves down before him. "We are your slaves," they said. But Joseph said to them, "Don't be afraid. Am I in the place of God? You intended to harm me, but God intended it for good to accomplish what is now being done, the saving

of many lives."

This is something that we have got to come to grips with at some point: that what was intended against Joseph in this context of evil—to bring this guy down, to eliminate him, to humiliate him, to ruin him—God intended to turn around and make it useful for something good.

And what the brothers saw as taking out vengeance on Joseph, God saw as preparing salvation for Israel and saving many lives through one of his children.

And as the perception of the brothers was that their intent was for evil, Joseph's wisdom in his relationship with God helped him see that what he was going through was intended by God for good.

That's what was taking place. God was making good out of what we, in the flesh, could not possibly perceive as good. How could it be good to be sold? How could it be good to be falsely accused? How could it be good to be thrown into jail? How can those things be good? Because God was working on a plan that was so far beyond the perception of man.

God was making good happen out of what could not possibly have been seen as good.

And Joseph's revelation was this: "This is the hand of God, and it doesn't matter what you intended to do to me because God intended to use it to bless other people. God had a plan to make it good."

That was the plan of God.

We quote Romans 8:28 all the time, but I want you to read it again:

> *And we know that in all things, God works for the good of those who love him, who have been called according to his purpose.*

"And we know." This is something that we *know*. We don't wonder. We don't consider it. We *know* it. That's an assurance of what's to follow: "We know that in all things." How many are there? It doesn't matter where you're from; **all means all**. "We know that in all things, God works for the good." God is causing good to come out of all things. How many things? All things. How big is your trial? How bad is your trial? Well, the answer is: It doesn't matter how big it is, it doesn't matter how bad it is, and it doesn't matter how long it is because God will make it good.

That is His promise from Joseph's life, and the children of God are supposed to say, "We know this is true. We know it. We don't wonder. **_We know_**."

Yet, we have these trials and troubles in life, and we think, "Well, how can good come of this?" And if you say to yourself, "How can good come of this?" You don't fully understand this passage because God does not have to explain to us the intricacies of how He is going to make it good. To be honest, it's none of our business how he is going to do it.

We just feel like we're entitled to know the plan when, in truth, we're not. That's called trust. That's called faith. That is, we believe that God has our best interests in mind.

What we have to be assured of is that the Word of God is faithful and true. And what is bad will become good. Think of the things in your life right now that are not good. Just think of some of the things that you're going through. Remember this: that thing that you're thinking of will become good because that's the promise of God. <u>And the promises of God never fail</u>.

Now, I want to look at Esther 5. This is an intense story. You will get a whole Bible story in a few pages, but it's a great story.

There are several key players in the story. First, there's Esther and Mordecai. Esther and Mordecai are cousins. We know that Mordecai is older than Esther because he took her into his house and helped raise her when her parents passed on. Both of these two are of Jewish descent. They are in a land that doesn't have a lot of Jewish people. But there are some. There is always a deli.

There's another person involved in this story. His name is Haman. Haman is second in command under the king. Now, I want you to follow this. The king chose Esther to be his wife. In those times, the king had many wives—hundreds of wives. But the Scripture takes the time to point out that Esther was the king's favorite. He liked her more than anyone else.

Mordecai's claim to fame in the book is that he found out that there was a plot to assassinate the king. So he decided to have the information given to the king. Because of the information he gave the king, they were able to stop the assassination.

Now, Haman had a huge pride problem, and he loved that wherever he went, people bowed down in front of him because he was a powerful man. But there was one person who would not bow down in front of him: Mordecai.

Mordecai had no compromise in his bones. He wasn't going to bow to a man for anything, anywhere, or at any time. As a matter of fact, every time Haman went down the street, everybody would bow but one figure: Mordecai. He'd just be standing there with an expression like, "Hey, no way, pal. I'm not bowing to you. No way."

Because of this, Haman's anger really got a hold of him. He started to rage in the face and thought, "I just really want to make Mordecai's life miserable."

So, when he finds out that Mordecai is Jewish, he makes a plan. "What I'm going to do to get back at Mordecai is go beyond just killing him. I am also going to kill **all the Jews**. Every single one. Then Mordecai will be destroyed." This is the definition of vengeance.

And this is where we pick it up now, in Esther chapter 5:10:

> *Calling together his friends and Zeresh, his wife, Haman boasted to them about his vast wealth, his many sons, and all the ways the king had honored him and how he had elevated him above the other nobles and officials. "And that's not all," Haman added. "I'm the only person Queen Esther invited to accompany the king to the banquet she gave.*

And she has invited me, along with the king, tomorrow. But all this gives me no satisfaction as long as I see that Jew Mordecai is sitting at the king's gate." So his wife Zeresh and all his friends said to him, "Have a gallows built, seventy-five feet high, and ask the king in the morning to have Mordecai hanged on it. Then go with the king to dinner and be happy." This suggestion delighted Haman, and he had the gallows built.

Continuing in chapter 6: *"That night."* Now, watch what God does. Here's God. If you're Mordecai, **you don't know what's going on**, but it's not good, is it?

That night, the king could not sleep, so he ordered the book of the chronicles, the record of his reign, to be brought in and read to him. It was found and recorded there that Mordecai had exposed Bigthana and Teresh, two of the king's officers who guarded the doorway, who had conspired to assassinate King Xerxes. "What honor and recognition has Mordecai received for this?" the king asked. "Nothing has been done for him," his attendants answered.

> *The king said, "Who is in the court?" Now Haman had just entered the palace's outer court to speak to the king about hanging Mordecai on the gallows he had erected for him.*

Can you say, "Bad timing?" I think Haman can.

> *His attendants answered, "Haman is standing in the court." "Bring him in," the king ordered. When Haman entered, the king asked him, "What should be done for the man the king delights to honor?" Now Haman thought to himself, "Who is there that the king would rather honor than me?" So he answered the king, "For the man, whom the king delights to honor, have them bring a royal robe the king has worn and a horse the king has ridden, one with a royal crest placed on its head. Then let the robe and horse be entrusted to one of the king's most noble princes. Let them robe the man the king delights to honor and lead him on the horse through the city streets, proclaiming before him, 'This is what is done for the man the king delights to honor!'"*

Now, Haman's trying to jazz it up for himself.

*"Go at once," the king commanded Haman. "Get the robe and the horse and do just as you have suggested **for Mordecai the Jew, who sits at the king's gate.** Do not neglect anything you have recommended." So Haman got the robe and the horse. He robed Mordecai and led him on horseback through the city streets, proclaiming before him, "This is what is done for the man the king delights to honor!"*

Afterward, Mordecai returned to the king's gate. But Haman rushed home, with his head covered, in grief, and told Zeresh, his wife, and all his friends everything that had happened to him. Then, his advisers and his wife Zeresh said to him, "Since Mordecai, before whom your downfall has started, is of Jewish origin, you cannot stand against him.

"You will surely come to ruin!" Then, while they were still talking with him, the king's eunuchs arrived and hurried Haman away to the banquet Esther had prepared.

At this point, Haman is just humiliated.

So the king and Haman went to dine with Queen Esther, and as they were drinking wine on that second day, the king again asked, "Queen Esther, what is your petition? It will be given to you. What is your request? Even up to half the kingdom, it will be granted." Then Queen Esther answered, "If I have found favor with you, O king, and if it pleases your majesty, grant me my life—this is my petition. And spare my people— this is my request, for me and my people have been sold for destruction, slaughter, and annihilation. If we had merely been sold as male and female slaves, I would have kept quiet, because no such distress would justify disturbing the king." King Xerxes asked Queen Esther, "Who is he? Where is the man who has dared to do such a thing?"

<u>Haman didn't realize that Esther was Jewish.</u> **Whoops!** <u>It is a small oversight.</u>

Esther said, "The adversary and enemy is this vile Haman." So then Haman was terrified before the king and queen.

The king got up in a rage, left his wine, and went out into the palace garden. But Haman, realizing that the king had already decided his fate, stayed behind to beg Queen Esther for his life. Just as the king returned from the palace garden to the banquet hall, Haman was falling on the couch where Esther was reclining. The king exclaimed, "Will he even molest the queen while she is with me in the house?"

Haman is having a terrible day.

As soon as the word left the king's mouth, they covered Haman's face. Then Harbona, one of the eunuchs attending the king, said, "A gallows seventy-five feet high stands by Haman's house. He had it made for Mordecai, who spoke up to help the king." The king said, "Hang him on it!"

Look at what happened in this story. The enemy of the people of God had set up a plan to wipe out the people of God. And the plan seemed brilliant, <u>and it should have</u> <u>worked</u>. When the Jews heard about the plan to kill them, they became distressed. Things were looking bad. **But God had a plan all along**. That one sleepless night for the king completely changed the fate of the nation of Israel. This is so powerful.

The very thing that Haman had intended to do was the very thing that was done to him. Look at verse 10: *"So they hanged Haman on the gallows he had prepared for Mordecai."* The very thing that the enemy sets up to use against the very people of God is the very thing that God is going to use to kill the enemy.

The same is true in your life. God is going to turn the very things that have been set up to bring destruction into your life around so that those things set up to hurt you will end up hurting the enemy instead. They are not going to destroy you, even though you will feel (at times) the dread, the scare, and even the uncomfortableness of the warfare. God is going to turn it around before the crucial moment of disaster.

And you will not be stuck on some gallows 75 feet high. Still, your enemies—the enemies that try to crush your Christian faith, the enemies that try to rob your very existence—will be hung on the gallows, not you. God will turn it around, and it will never be the same.

Even though you'll feel how close the gallows might come, God will not let the noose around your neck be lifted. Instead, he will stop it before it takes place. Mr. Eleventh Hour, Mr. In the Nick of Time.

Let's look at Psalm 30:4-5. This is so wonderful.

> *Sing to the LORD, you saints of his; praise his holy name. For his anger lasts only a moment, but his favor lasts a lifetime; weeping may remain for a night, but rejoicing comes in the morning.*

Now, look at verse 11 of the same Psalm. "*You turned my wailing into dancing; you removed my sackcloth, and you clothed me with joy.*" God will take the things in your life that are causing sorrow—that are creating mourning and frustration—and He will turn them around so that you will be able to dance in the might of the Lord.

You will be able to see the trial as both a strength and a power. It will not beat you down, but it will lift you up. It was set up to bring you into death, but it will end up giving you life because God will take the things that make us wail, and He will cause them to make us dance.

Is that powerful or what? That's the power of God. **And it's in your life.**

Now, let's look at Acts 26:9-18. This is one of my favorite passages of Scripture:

> *"I too was convinced that I ought to do all that was possible to oppose the name of Jesus of Nazareth. And that is just what I did in Jerusalem. On the authority of the chief*

priests, I put many of the saints in prison, and when they were put to death, I cast my vote against them. Many a time, I went from one synagogue to another to have them punished, and I tried to force them to blaspheme. In my obsession with them, I even went to foreign cities to persecute them.

"On one of these journeys, I was going to Damascus with the authority and commission of the chief priests. About noon, O King, as I was on the road, I saw a light from heaven, brighter than the sun, blazing around me and my companions. We all fell to the ground, and I heard a voice saying to me in Aramaic, 'Saul, Saul, why do you persecute me? It is hard for you to kick against the goads.' "Then I asked, 'Who are you, Lord?' "I am Jesus, whom you are persecuting,' the Lord replied. 'Now get up and stand on your feet. I have appeared to you to appoint you as a servant and as a witness to what you have seen of me and what I will show you. I will rescue you from your own people and from the Gentiles. I am sending you to them to open their eyes and turn them from darkness to light and from the power of Satan to God, so that they may receive forgiveness of sins and a place among those who are sanctified by faith in me.'

The very person that the devil instituted to destroy the church is the same person that God instituted to build it higher than anyone could have imagined.

Only God.

The man who was ordained by the enemy to rip it apart—to go through and bring oppression and to beat people down and to have them killed—is the very man whom God used to write the majority of the New Testament, to help lay the foundation with the apostles, and to lay out a Christian faith and a way that we can walk in it intimately.

The man that the enemy tried to use to destroy Christians is God's man to give Christians life.

What the enemy tries to use in your life to destroy you, God will use to build you up. Did you see that? **That's the key**. What the enemy tries to use to destroy you, God will use to build you up. This is such a powerful insight.

It's so good I am going to repeat it (on purpose): What the enemy tries to use in your life to destroy you, God will use it to build you up. Did you see that? **That's the key**. What the enemy tries to use to destroy you, God will use to build you up. This is a powerful insight.

In closing, I have a question to ask God. Why? Why do you turn things around? Why do you take what is absolutely certain death in our minds and make it life? Why do you take the Sauls in our lives and make them become Pauls? Why do you take the gallows that are meant for us and put our enemy's neck in them? Why, when we think it's all only evil, are you making it all good?

Let's close the chapter by taking a look at Psalm 18:1-19:

> *I love you, O LORD, my strength. The LORD is my rock, my fortress, and my deliverer; my God is my rock, in whom I take refuge. He is my shield, the horn of my salvation, and my stronghold. So I call to the LORD, who is worthy of praise, and I am saved from my enemies.*
>
> *The cords of death entangled me, and the torrents of destruction overwhelmed me. The cords of the grave coiled around me; the snares of death confronted me. In my distress, I called to the LORD; I cried to my God for help. From his temple, he heard my voice; my cry came before him, into his ears.*

The earth trembled and quaked, and the foundations of the mountains shook. They trembled because he was angry. Smoke rose from his nostrils; consuming fire came from his mouth; burning coals blazed out of it. He parted the heavens and came down; dark clouds were under his feet. He mounted the cherubim and flew; he soared on the wings of the wind. He made darkness his covering, his canopy around him—the dark rain clouds of the sky.

Out of the brightness of his presence, clouds advanced, with hailstones and bolts of lightning. The LORD thundered from heaven, and the voice of the Most High resounded. He shot his arrows, scattered the enemies with great bolts of lightning, and routed them. The valleys of the sea were exposed, and the foundations of the earth were laid bare at your rebuke, O LORD, at the blast of breath from your nostrils.

He reached down from high and took hold of me; <u>he drew me out of deep waters</u>. He rescued me from my powerful enemy and from my foes, who were too strong for me. They confronted me on the day of my disaster, but the Lord was my support. He brought me out

> *into a spacious place; he rescued me because he delighted in me.*

Do you want to know why God does this stuff? **_He does it because he loves us._** He looks down from heaven, and he says, "Those are my kids. Stop it."

And He comes down in fury, and He changes things.

That is exactly what Psalm 18 teaches.

God sees the things that are going on in our lives. He sees the distress, and it irritates Him as it irritates us. He gets aggravated, and He stretches down His hand to earth and says, **"It's not going to stay that way."**

And that's how He makes all things work together for good. He will not let life's circumstances and our enemies whip us down and beat us up. <u>After all, we are His kids,</u> and <u>*He loves us.*</u> <u>He has a passion for us.</u>

I want you to read Matthew 23:37. This is Jesus speaking:

> *"O Jerusalem, Jerusalem, you who kill the prophets and stone those sent to you, how often I have longed to gather your children together, as a hen gathers her chicks under her wings."*

Listen to what Jesus is saying. He is saying, "Jerusalem, My people, the reason that you are even in existence, I have longed to come to you and to put My arms around you and to pull you into my chest and to hug you and to love on you and to kiss your face and to let you know how much passion I have for you.

Jerusalem, my children, my people, where are you? All I want to do is put my arms around you. You don't have to be perfect. You'll never be perfect. But I want you. I want you as my kids. I want you as my own. I want that relationship. I want that intimacy."

Most of us spend a lifetime looking for some sense of intimacy, some sense of deliverance, some sense of love, and God is there on the spot every moment, desiring, deep in His heart, to take His arms and stretch them around us and pull us close to His side, and to kiss us on the forehead and say, "I love you."

We spend so much of our lives looking to other people and other things for the love that God longs to pour into us. Whenever we get it from any other place other than God, it doesn't work, does it? It doesn't last.

You know it, and I know it. And most of us know it from experience. It just doesn't work. If it's not the arms of the Lord, it doesn't work.

Why does Jesus do all of these things? Because He loves us. He said to Israel, *"I've desired to gather you like chicks under her wings, but you were not willing."*

That had to be one of the harshest moments for Jesus as he looked at Israel. He knew what was going to happen. And he did it all because he loved them. But they were not willing to receive his love. So, little did they know they were about to go through hell.

A little more than thirty-five years later, Jerusalem was annihilated. There wasn't a stone left in the temple. God wanted to love Israel. **They needed that love, but they weren't willing to receive it from God**.

We are all going to suffer in this life. There are going to be those harsh moments when we just want to give up. But the Lord will take what's harsh in your life and smooth it out. He will take what is bad, and he will make it good. He will take what is bad, and he will make it rad.

He will take the worst and make it the best because He loves us.

We cannot be like Jerusalem. We cannot turn away.

We must hear His cry, "I want to love you. Let me love you." So, let's put ourselves in a place where we will acknowledge and desire God's love for us, and stop running from Him.

10

Finding the Will of God

It is amazing how many self-help books are in society today. Have you ever heard of the "OK" series?

I'm OK; You're OK.

I'm OK. You're not so OK.

I'm not so OK. I don't like you. I'm OK. You're a Jerk.

That's the way all these self-help books keep leading people. These books promote the idea that you are going to find self-discovery by reading a book that some people wrote. Have you ever met anybody who was as good as God? Not a chance! Who is going to write a book that's so good that you're going to "discover yourself" because of the book that you read?

The Bible says, *"Let God be true, and every man a liar."* That qualifies all the authors of self-help books to be liars. So why would you think that a self-help book is going to change you?

Better yet, there is an entire subcategory of Christian self-help books. There are. But there are two problems with that. <u>First</u>, some of them are self-help books, and the problem is that we already spend so much time focused on ourselves.

<u>Second</u>, there are also Christian ministers (so-called) who will tell you: "Listen, you know, you're ok. Everything is great. As long as you support my ministry, you don't need to worry. God will bless you. God will be with you. God will show you." Have you ever run into these people? You probably think I'm kidding. Christians are sometimes the worst when it comes to self-help.

For instance, a minister made a promise to everyone who sent a donation. They would receive a unique present. They would receive "his" book. A special book. One that he "anointed" himself. It's a good thing that the minister anointed it, not the Holy Spirit. Get it?

The minister said that if they sent him the $29.95 donation, he would send them this anointed book (by him), along with something that would absolutely, positively guarantee that they would never be penniless as long as they held on to it for the rest of their lives. Do you know what he sent along with his book? It was a penny.

That is shameful. Completely shameful.

Do you think that a Christian author is going to **have a better understanding** of your self-discovery and your purpose in life **than God**, the author of life?

Do you think anybody could ever write a book that could live up to God's own words in the Scriptures? Absolutely not.

I know there are some really good books out there. Some books start off great and then slowly move into a little bit of legalism. So there are all kinds of books that are all over the place. Like this one, you are reading right now. But do you know what? If I want to know what my self-discovery issues are, <u>I want to hear from the person who is the author of life, my Creator.</u>

Please absorb what I am about to write. *Life is a waste unless we discover the purpose of our creation.* Only the Creator can define what this purpose is. **God defines our purpose for our lives through the revelation of His will.**

Let's take a look at Colossians 1:9. It says this:

> *For this reason, since the day we heard about you, we have not stopped praying for you and asking God to fill you with the knowledge of his will through all spiritual wisdom and understanding.*

God wants you to know what His will is for your life. Ephesians 5:17 says this: "*Therefore do not be foolish but understand what the Lord's will is.*" God wants us to know what His will is.

We need to understand something first, though. **There is a *general will*, and there is a *specific will*.**

First, let's talk about the general will of God. God's general will must include things we all know and love to be true regarding what God wants us to do.

Matthew 4:1-3 says this:

> *Then Jesus was led by the Spirit into the desert to be tempted by the devil. After fasting for forty days and forty nights, he was hungry. The tempter came to him and said, "If you are the Son of God, tell these stones to become bread." Jesus answered, "It is written: 'Man does not live on bread alone, but on every word*

that comes from the mouth of God."

The first will that I want to tell you about in the general will of God is that the Bible is equated to bread. It's our food. We need it for survival. Jesus said, *"Man does not live by bread alone, but by every word that proceeds out of the mouth of God."* So God tells us His will is to live by what His Word has to say.

If you really examine that passage, there are some great insights because what the devil does right off the bat is say, *"If Thou be the Son of God."* He says to Jesus, "Well, if you're Him." <u>The devil is a master at self-doubt</u>. And he tried it on the Son of God. "If you are really the Son of God."

I'm sure Jesus was thinking, "Oh, are you in for a treat."

But look at this. He is telling us that the Word of God is like bread. So, if we want to be in God's general will, the first thing we need to do is be in the Word of God. This is **numero uno** on the will of God stuff. We can't survive without that sustenance.

The second will of God is for us to pray, spend time with God, talk to Him, and practice our dependence on Him.

Let's look at Philippians 4:6. Paul writes, "*Do not be anxious about anything, but in everything, by prayer and petition, with thanksgiving, present your requests to God.*" Don't be anxious about anything but prayer (<u>which</u> <u>declares our dependence</u>) and **petition**. The word "petition" in the NIV means a specific need.

Prayer in this context can be defined like this: *dependence on and acknowledgment of God in communication.* And it's asking for a specific need. It's an attitude of gratitude, and it's asking for a specific desire. And what Paul says is: "Hey, you should pray...be anxious for nothing, but instead pray about everything."

The third will of God is fellowship. Let's look at Hebrews 10:25:

> *"Let us not give up meeting together, as some are in the habit of doing, but let us encourage one another—and all the more as you see the Day approaching."*

So, the third will of God for your life is fellowship. Don't give up meeting together. Don't do that.

Why is fellowship so important? Because you, as an individual Christian, away from all other Christians, are an easy target. It's easy for Satan to pick us off. It is easy for him to dump on us. It's easy to make us feel like garbage. We go to your church once a week; we hear the Word for about thirty minutes. Then we walk out thinking, "Yeah, man, I could do better than I'm doing. I've got God on my side." It encourages us. Well, that's what it's supposed to do. That's the will of God for your life.

The fourth will, in God's general will, is a little tougher. Remember the shameful minister? Yeah...he's not helping. 2 Corinthians 9:6 says this:

> *Remember this: Whoever sows sparingly will also reap sparingly, and whoever sows generously will also reap generously. Each man should give what he has decided in his heart to give, not reluctantly or under compulsion, for God loves a cheerful giver. And God is able to make all grace abound to you, so that in all things at all times, having all that you need, you will abound in every good work.*

The fourth realm of the will of God is for you to be a giver. We have a lot of people who give like this: "Okay, God, here's your 10%." <u>But do you actually think God needs your money</u>? You've got to be kidding me. As an older brother in the Lord, I think it would be great if somebody came in and dropped a million dollars into our ministry. But a lack of money isn't going to stop God's plan from moving forward. If the kingdom is the will of God, it's going to carry on.

The truth is this: **God doesn't need your money. He** wants your heart.

Some people are so attached to their money that they can't separate the two. That's a sign of the wrong attitude. But God wants us to give cheerfully. And what if you can't give money? That's fine. Give your time or your talent. That's valuable. Ministries will gladly use the help.

The point is that we need to be giving something to God. But we also need to give with the right attitude. Why does God want us to give? Because He is a giver (John 3:16), He wants you to follow in His tracks.

What's another will of God in your life? <u>To serve in the body to help build each other up</u>. Ephesians 4:11 says this: *"It was he who gave some to be apostles, some to be prophets, some to be evangelists, and some to be pastors and teachers."* And why did he organize things this way? Verse 12: **"to EQUIP God's people."**

Stop! Who are God's people? That's you, right? Read this again: *"to equip God's people for works of service...works of service so that the body of*

Christ may be built up." That's YOU!

In America, the people who do what I'm doing are all called professional ministers. I'm not too fond of the term *professional minister.* What's a professional minister? What does that mean? That's absurd.

Do you remember the story about the guy who had all the evil spirits in him and Jesus casting all those spirits out of that guy? The one that had the evil spirit was named Legion. After Jesus casts the demons out of the man, the man says something to the effect of, "Hey, I want to come hang out with you."

What did Jesus say? He said, "No. You go tell everybody what happened."

If that guy was in the church today and Jesus cast those spirits out of him, he would be required to go to 50 classes of preparation before he could go witness to anybody. Then he'd have to go through church membership. Then, the church would make him jump through a ton of hoops before they'd allow him to do any ministry.

But what did Jesus do? Jesus just said, "Go. Go tell them what I did."

The sixth will of God is for us all to be **reachers**.

Reaching the lost and the unchurched. This area is the one I love the most. 2 Corinthians 5:18 says this: "*All this is from God, who reconciled us to himself through Christ and gave us the ministry of reconciliation.*"

To whom did He give the ministry of reconciliation? **He gave it to us**. He gave us the ministry of reconciliation, saying that *"God was reconciling the world to himself in Christ, not counting men's sins against them. And he has committed to us the message of reconciliation. We are, therefore, Christ's ambassadors, as though God were making his appeal through us.*"

God gave the message to us through Christ. Now, it's our message to give to others who need to hear it.

Many people think they are Christians because they think that Jesus is real, but they don't know anything about Him or the kingdom. They've not been through a Bible study. They've not experienced a real prayer session. I have not heard a decent sermon. They just know Jesus is real, and they don't know anything else. Those are unchurched (and many unsaved) people.

It is our job to reconcile, reach out to them, reconcile the lost, bring that message to the lost, and bring those who are unchurched into a developing relationship with God. That's part of the will of God for our lives. So, just who did He give the ministry of reconciliation to? Us.

It's our ministry now.

The last general will of God that I want to show you is impossible to miss. If you miss this, I can't help you. Are you ready? 1 Thessalonians 5:18: "*Give thanks in all circumstances, for this is God's will for you in Christ Jesus.*"

I cannot say anything to this that can make it any clearer in any possible capacity. "***Give thanks in all circumstances, for this is God's will for you in Christ Jesus.***"

Do you want to know what God's will is? God's will is not to think, "I don't like the way you do it, Jesus." God's will for us is not to be whiners or complainers.

Remember the children of Israel and how well that went for them? <u>But the idea here is for us to be thankful</u> <u>for all things</u>. Why? Because God loves you. He's not just going to let you hang out there to dry. He's not going to leave you in the lurch. What kind of God would that be?

<u>So, what is God's general will for us</u>? First, He wants us to have a passion for the Word (**1**). Second, He wants us to have a passion for prayer (**2**). Third, He wants us to be in fellowship (**3**). Fourth, He wants us to be givers (**4**). Fifth, He wants us to be servants (**5**). Sixth, He wants us to be people who reach the lost and the unchurched (**6**). And Seventh, He wants us to be thankful (**7**).

Now, it's time to turn it up a notch and blow your minds a little. You've got to know the general will of God. **But there is also a specific will of God for each and every one of you**. And I'm going to tell you what that is today, right now. I'm going to tell you what the specific will of God is for your life <u>because you have an individual ministry, an individual purpose, and an individual calling</u>. That specific will of God is for you alone, with nobody else attached to its ownership but you.

Ephesians 4:16 says this:

> *"From him, the whole body, joined and held together by every supporting ligament, grows and builds itself up in love, as each part does its work."*

I really want to emphasize this: **Only you have a ministry with your fingerprints on it, and nobody else's**. Everybody reading this book has an individual, specific call that God has requested in their life. Let's look at one more passage, and then I'll tell you how to find God's will for you specifically. Let's look at Acts 26 because I want you to see how important this is to the Kingdom of God. You don't have to spend billions of dollars trying to figure this out from all those self-help books. Our Creator has made it simple. He put it right here in His Word.

Here is Paul speaking in Acts 26:12-16:

"I was going to Damascus with the authority and commission of the chief priests. About noon, O King, as I was on the road, I saw a light from heaven, brighter than the sun, blazing around me and my companions. We all fell to the ground, and I heard a voice saying to me in Aramaic, 'Saul, Saul, why do you persecute me? It is hard for you to kick against the goads.' "Then I asked, 'Who are you, Lord? 'I am Jesus, whom you are persecuting,' the Lord replied. Now get up and stand on your feet. I have appeared to you to appoint you as a servant and as a witness."

The Greek word for "**appoint you**" means "**choose you for this**." That's exactly what He's saying. _The point is that it is a specific assignment._ God has a specific assignment for each and every one of us. So, how do we find the specific assignment? I'm going to give you a practical, step-by-step method to find out exactly what God wants you to do. Ready?

The first thing that we need to know in order to find the specific will of God is to read James 1:5. James 1:5 says:

> *"If any of you lacks wisdom, he should ask God, who gives generously to all without finding fault, and it will be given to him."*

This is a real mystery. So first, we need to ask God. You see, the Creator created you, and He has given you a specific purpose and a specific plan, so it makes sense to start this process off by asking Him, "What is it? What's your purpose for me?"

Doesn't that make sense? So, we need to ask God, "Well, what is it? What's your purpose for me?" **That's what God wants you to do**. So, he wants you to start off by asking.

And He doesn't want you to be afraid to ask because He promises to give generously to you and give you answers without finding fault. If He wanted to pick you apart, He could. But he's not looking to do that. He's looking for you to come to Him and seek His counsel, wisdom, and advice.

The second thing that we need to know in order to find the specific will of God is found in Isaiah 6:8:

"Then I heard the voice of the Lord saying, 'Whom shall I send? And who will go for us?' And I said, 'Here am I. Send me!'"

The first thing you do is ask God, "What is my purpose?" The second thing that you do is go, "You know what, Lord? Here I am to fulfill whatever that is." The first one is inquiring. The second one is presenting. "Here I am. Tell me. I will do whatever you want."

Third, let's look at Romans 12:2. It says: "Do not conform any longer to the pattern of this world, but be transformed by the renewing of your mind." Watch this. *"Then you will be able to test and approve what God's will is—his good, pleasing and perfect will."*

The first thing you do is ask God (**1**). The second thing you do is present yourself (**2**). And the third thing you do is keep your mind renewed so you can be spiritually minded (**3**).

Listen, I've got a message for you: **The purpose of your creation isn't for your flesh to be all happy**. It's not for you to sin your brains out. That's not why you were created. Instead, the purpose of your creation is spiritually oriented, so we need to be spiritually minded.

The fourth key to discovering God's specific will for you is found in John 4:34: "'*My food,' said Jesus, 'is to do the will of him who sent me and to finish his work.*'" My food," Jesus said. <u>What Jesus did was declare that the will of the Father was His top priority</u>.

We ask (**1**). We present ourselves (**2**). We are spiritually minded (**3**). We make His will a top priority (**4**).

Here's the final point: It has been biblically declared that God's specific will for your life "often" coincides with a person's deepest personal passions.

Isn't that contrary to what you have been telling us?

Not if it is <u>God doing the planting</u> of the passions.

This is illustrated clearly in Philippians 2:13: "*For it is God who works in you to will and to act according to his good purpose.*" So let me take you a little further and explain it. God works in you **to will** and **to act** according to His good purpose. The Greek word here for "will" is to desire. And the word "act" is to perform.

Let me read it with the mindset of what Paul would have said to us.

"For it is God who works in you to desire and to perform according to His good purpose (my paraphrase)."

Do you want to know the specific will of God in your life? Well, guess what happened when you were created? God put a seed in you. It's this deep seed in your heart. And God, in putting that in you, has the seed (the idea) work its way to the surface. It's what God's plan is for you specifically, and it turns out that that seed is what you would desire deep in your heart.

So listen to what the verse says: *God works in you to desire.* He is working in you **for you to desire** and then **to perform** according to His plan. This isn't your flesh saying I want to be a gazillionaire. God's plans for you coincide with His plans for kingdom building. ALWAYS!!!

You see, God wants to work in partnership and in concert with each one of us. So what He does is, according to His will, He puts this seed in you that's for His purpose, His plan, and His glory.

But it turns out that's what you want to do anyway.

AMAZING!

Then, all of a sudden, we start to think, "Well, what I'm doing is no longer like work. I'm fulfilling my purpose." **That's it, right there**. You see, what nobody says is this: He put that seed inside of you.

And you think, "Well, OK. How do I get it?"

I will tell you: Close the door and ask God to pull it out of you because it's already buried deep inside you.

And a great practical way to start is to say, "Well, if I had $50 million and didn't have a care in the world, what would I do?"

Maybe it's a ministry format like singing. Maybe it's writing. Maybe it's crafting. Maybe it's sports. Maybe it's coaching. Maybe it's preaching. Maybe it's teaching. Maybe it's building Legos. I don't know because God put something unique inside each one of us. It's inside of you, so you have to say, "God, pull the seed out. Show me what it is. Let me do it."

When you discover the seed and ask God to grow it in your life, you're fulfilling your purpose of your personal creation because God's the one who made you that way. Bingo. Mic drop.

Do you know what I love to do? I love to teach. I love to write. I love the radio ministry that I do. I love counseling. I love all those things; if I had $50 million, that's all I would do.

Well, guess what? I don't have $50 million, but I'm still doing it. I'm still fulfilling my purpose. And I feel more alive doing this than anything. Why? Because it is what I was designed to do. It's in the depths of me.

And what is in the depths of you is what God put inside you for His purpose. So you have to ask God to pull it out. Some of you already know what I'm talking about.

You're just so afraid. You're so afraid of being happy. You're just so afraid that you'll like it. And you think you don't deserve that. Yet God put in you, inside of you, the very purpose of your creation.

So find it. Spend time with God and find it. Ask Him. Present yourself. Make yourself available. Be spiritually minded. Make it a top priority and search for it because it's already there.

And do you know what? **It doesn't matter what it is**. If God puts it in there, it will be for His glory, even if you can't figure it out right away. It's in you for a reason, and it's yours. That's what you are. It just needs to be unleashed. So ask God to help you uncover that seed in your life, and you'll be amazed at what happens in your life. Don't be afraid to be blessed.

The Lawsuit Gospel

You are going to read a theory you have not heard before.

It is called the lawsuit theory.

So here's the deal: God said if you sin, you have to die. That's the rule. Don't eat that fruit, Adam and Eve, because if you do, you're going to die, first spiritually and then physically. Every person has sinned, and every person has died.

Now, what happened to Jesus? Jesus didn't sin. He never sinned, but he still died. So he got hosed. He was not supposed to die. He didn't sin; therefore, He shouldn't have died.

I want to make sure you get this.

All people sin, and they have or will die. Jesus didn't sin, and he still died. So, he got the wrong end of the deal. So, do you know what he did? **He sued**.

In His lawsuit, He asked that everybody who believes in Him get His righteous life. Everybody who acknowledges Him gets His righteousness put on them. And that's what he sued for.

That's the gospel (The Good News) in a lawsuit.

Jesus announced, "I died, but I wasn't supposed to die, so there's a wrong in that. There's an injustice here, so I am suing the universe. Everybody who believes in Me (Jesus) receives what I should have had: eternal life through My eternal righteousness."

Then God the Father slammed down the gavel, and the case was closed. Judgment for the plaintiff. And the devil's whimpering, "Now hold on just a second," but it was too late.

All who have faith in Jesus Christ get the righteousness of Christ. That's the Lawsuit Theory of the Gospel. The Gospel is extremely judicial because God is a righteous judge, but Jesus died unjustly. And that wrong had to be righted. Remember, you only die if you sin, and Jesus didn't sin.

You are part of the award. That's what's so fantastic about God. Don't miss what the purpose is. God is not experimenting with people in a petri dish. The Lord wants to fellowship with us. He made it so that we could.

You don't know what's going to happen in one minute from now, let alone one hour from now. And God (who cannot lie) has made this commitment, made this offer, and made this opportunity for both you and me and all the people around us.

The simplicity is that all have sinned and fall short of the glory of God. The wages of that sin, the wages of falling short, are death. But the free gift of God is eternal life in Christ Jesus, our Lord. Thus, God demonstrates His love for us, Jesus Christ, to die for us while we were still sinners. And if you believe in your heart and confess with your mouth that Jesus is Lord, **you will be saved**. For God so loved the world that He gave His one and only Son that whoever believes in Him should not perish but have eternal life.

There is nothing more important than that principle right there. This hope is offered to believers who acknowledge and surrender to the testimony of Jesus Christ. That's what's being offered. That's what gives you encouragement. That's what enables you to go on.

You're going to have a lot of sorrow in this life. Job said it best. *A man's days are few and full of trouble.* But there is something so wonderful that even in man's mind, we cannot entertain the depth of it.

> *But, as it is written, "What no eye has seen, nor ear heard, nor the heart of man imagined, what God has prepared for those who love him"—*

We can't even understand what great things God has prepared for those of us who love Him. There's such a fantastic thing that's coming for us. Such a great place. Such a wondrous place. But you must acknowledge the invitation. You have got to say yes. Because if you don't say yes, you're not going to that wedding. The wedding of the lamb. Don't be that person. Don't be that person who rejects it. Don't be that person who always lives in sorrow, grief, or sadness.

Don't be that person.

Be the person who says yes. Then, you can be a part of the great wedding feast and the great celebration. Life is much more than this: 60, 70, 80, 90 years. It's been an eternity online. If you have already said yes, then rest in that comfort. Rest in that place. Rest in that goodness. All is well. And even on this side, if it's hard, on the other side, it's glorious.

Jesus brought life and immortality to light through the gospel. Through the gospel, Jesus died on the cross, was buried, and three days later, he rose again. And by faith in the testimony of God, you can live forever.

That hope is offered to us. That hope is offered to you. And if you have not yet accepted it, acknowledge it and surrender to it. I ask you to do so right now. I don't even care if you do a fancy prayer or say, "Please God save me in Jesus' name," you will be saved. If you believe that Jesus Christ died on the cross, was buried, and three days later, He rose again. You need to surrender your heart to Jesus Christ, turning from where you are right now to Him, and then <u>you will find life</u>! Eternal life.

You might be out there thinking that there's no way it can be that easy. Wrong! But you have to receive it; you have to surrender to it; you have to acknowledge God's testimony and say yes to Jesus Christ.

It doesn't matter what the world says; it doesn't matter what your friends say; it doesn't matter what other family members say. The only thing that matters is your decision before God regarding His testimony relating to Jesus Christ and your sins.

And that's the hope that is offered to us. We can be greatly encouraged by that. Hope is an anchor to our soul. That anchor makes it so that we don't get tossed around, even if the winds are heavy and the waves are intense. There is great stability there. There is access to enduring strength. You can't be like those people who have no hope. All they have is this life right now. There's nothing else for them. So that's why they're trying to sin their brains out.

They don't think there's anything else left. But they are wrong, and they are going to die and face God.

He's going to ask them to give an account of their lives. And they're going to have to answer to Him if they have rejected Jesus. <u>And so will you</u>. Then they will be as they have positioned themselves, as people with no hope. If you're a person who has not made the decision to say yes to Jesus Christ, make that decision right now.

PRAY THIS PRAYER...

> *Heavenly Father, I surrender my life. Lord Jesus Christ, I give you my heart. Pour out your Holy Spirit, for I believe that You rose from the dead, and I confess with my mouth that You died for my sins (according to the Scriptures), You were buried, and three days*

later... you rose again. You have ascended to the Father and are coming back soon! I thank you for this new life you have given me. I praise You and pray this...in Your name. Amen

Welcome to the family!

What's it all About?

The Purpose of Human Creation

Genesis 1-3 >>> [Not an experiment] **To Fellowship with and glorify God**

The Bad News: In the garden, Sin City >>> We lost it all!

But...There's Gospel "Good News" >>> Through Jesus, the sin is in the bin.

> 1) God **"Desires"** to be with *us*! Matthew 1:22-23

> 2) He even became "One of Us" Philippians 2:4-11

God loves us. John 3:16

(No, He doesn't have to), and...**He likes us too!**

Would you spend eternity with someone you didn't like?

So, what is Christianity?

Christianity is a living relationship with a living God that's made possible through the redeeming work of Jesus Christ and lived in the empowerment of the Holy Spirit.

It is the restoration of the original purpose of our creation!

The Four Spiritual Laws

1. God loves you.

   "For God so loved the world, that He gave His only begotten Son, that whoever believes in Him should not perish, but have eternal life" (John 3:16).

2. Man is sinful and separated from God.

   "For all have sinned and fall short of the glory of God" (Rom. 3:23). "For the wages of sin is death" (Rom. 6:23). "But your iniquities have made a separation between you and your God" (Isaiah 59:2).

3. Jesus Christ is God's only provision for man's sin.

   "I am the way, and the truth, and the life; no one comes to the Father, but through Me" (John 14:6). "But God demonstrates His own love toward us, in that while we were yet sinners, Christ died for us" (Rom. 5:8).

4. We must individually receive Jesus as Savior and Lord.

   "But as many as received Him, to them He gave the right to become children of God, even to those who believe in His name" (John 1:12). "If you confess with your mouth Jesus as Lord and believe in your heart that God raised Him from the dead, you shall be saved" (Rom. 10:9). "For by grace you have been saved through faith; and that not of yourselves, it is the gift of God" (Eph. 2:8).

The Roman's Road

1. Rom. 3:10, "As it is written, 'There is none righteous, not even one."

2. Rom. 3:23, "For all have sinned and fall short of the glory of God."

3. Rom. 5:12, "Therefore, just as through one man sin entered into the world, and death through sin, and so death spread to all men because all sinned."

4. Rom. 6:23, "For the wages of sin is death, but the free gift of God is eternal life in Christ Jesus our Lord."

5. Rom. 5:8, "But God demonstrates His own love toward us, in that while we were yet sinners, Christ died for us."

6. Rom. 10:9-10, "If you confess with your mouth Jesus as Lord and believe in your heart that God raised Him from the dead, you shall be saved; for with the heart man believes, resulting in righteousness, and with the mouth, he confesses, resulting in salvation."

7. Rom. 10:13, "For whoever will call upon the
    name of the Lord will be saved."

About this Jewish Christian

David Spoon was born and raised in a Jewish home in Detroit, Michigan. He attended a private Hebrew school called Hillel Hebrew Academy. David was bar mitzvahed at the age of thirteen. Not long after, he was involved in drug abuse and trafficking. After Hearing the gospel for the first time at age seventeen, David accepted Jesus Christ as his Lord and Savior. A few months later, David had a dramatic experience with God. Immediately set free from years of excessive drug use, he committed himself to ministry and to furthering the Kingdom of God.

He graduated from Life Pacific College summa-cum-laude in their Ministry and Leadership program. He also graduated with honors from Regent University with a Master's Degree in Theological Studies and completed his Doctor of Ministry program in Strategic Christian Ministry at Liberty University.

David is married to his best friend, Noelle. He has three children and seven grandchildren, plus a dog named Bert. On March 18th, 2019, he started "The David Spoon Experience" in Texas.

He is the President of He Must Increase Ministry, a 501c3 ministry and hosts the live daily radio show "The David Spoon Experience" through DJR Broadcasting on the KAAM 770 A.M. radio dial, on various apps, as well as the Internet. David is a Jewish-Christian, Bapti-Costal, Cal-Minian, and Manifold Millennialist. Just ask him.

Also, by David Spoon

BROKEN... FOR HIS GLORY!

Not all Churches are Bad, but not all Churches are Good!

It is a book for anyone involved in a church as a servant, a leader, a member, or an attendee who now finds themselves misplaced, lost, confused, wandering, and just wondering, Why God?

Has a church burned you? Award-winning author, radio host, and former pastor Dr. David Spoon unveils his book "BROKEN FOR HIS GLORY" to investigate that very question.

Using his own painful church experience as a springboard for teaching others, Dr. Spoon spins his adolescent battles with drug addiction, eventual conversion to Christianity, and woundings at the hands of a church into a personal journey designed to help readers resolve and recover from their spiritual conflicts.

Connecting the stages of Jesus' sufferings to Christians who have experienced church pain and personal hurts, Dr. Spoon shows that being wounded isn't the end of the world. Instead, it can end up being a good thing.

www.ingramcontent.com/pod-product-compliance
Lightning Source LLC
Chambersburg PA
CBHW071414150726
48000CB00001B/323